I JUST SAW JESUS

Easter '89

Dave,

may we see Him more clearly,
so we might love Him more dearly!

Mike & Gay ann

I JUST SAW JESUS

by
Paul Eshleman

This special edition published by:

THE JESUS PROJECT
Campus Crusade for Christ
Arrowhead Springs
San Bernardino, CA 92414

I JUST SAW JESUS

By Paul Eshleman

with Carolyn E. Phillips

Published by
THE JESUS PROJECT
P.O. Box 7690
Laguna Niguel, CA 92677
(714) 495-7383

HLP Product No. 951111
© Campus Crusade for Christ
All rights reserved.
Printed in the United States of America.

Library of Congress Cataloging in Publication
Eshleman, Paul.

I Just Saw Jesus.

1. Moving-pictures in evangelistic work.
2. Jesus (Motion picture)
   I. Title.

BV3793.E84   1985   266   85-8712
ISBN 0-89840-100-3 (pbk.)

FOR MORE INFORMATION, WRITE:

L.I.F.E. — P.O. Box A399, Sydney South 2000, Australia
Campus Crusade for Christ of Canada — Box 300, Vancouver, B.C., V6C 2X3, Canada
Campus Crusade for Christ — 103 Friar Street, Reading RG1 1EP, Berkshire, England
Lay Institute for Evangelism — P.O. Box 8786, Auckland 3, New Zealand
Great Commission Movement of Nigeria — P.O. Box 500, Jos, Plateau State Nigeria, West Africa
Life Ministry — P.O. Box/Bus. 91015, Auckland Park 2006, Republic of South Africa
Campus Crusade for Christ International — Arrowhead Springs, San Bernardino, CA 92414, U.S.A.

CONTENTS

DEDICATION

It is with deep love and appreciation that this book is dedicated to Caroline and Bunker Hunt, John Heyman, and the thousands of staff and film team members who risk their lives daily to take *JESUS* to the ends of the earth.

FOREWORD

One of the most powerful tools God has given us to proclaim the gospel today is the medium of film. We live in an age dominated by the media, and since the early days of my ministry I have seen the way God has used films to reach people for Christ in every kind of culture.

In the pages of this book Paul Eshleman tells the fascinating story of the film called *JESUS*, which is a vivid portrayal of the life, death, and resurrection of Jesus using the exact words of the Bible. He recounts the way the film was produced and distributed, in spite of seemingly insurmountable odds. He also tells of lives that have been touched by the Lord through the *JESUS* film. This story needs to be told, and no one is better qualified to tell it than Paul Eshleman because of his personal experience with the film.

In Matthew 24 Jesus declared that prior to His second coming to earth the gospel of the Kingdom would be preached to the whole world. Perhaps God is using this film, *JESUS*, as one of the means to hasten the day when "every knee shall bow" before our great King.

JESUS has been translated into many languages. Millions have seen it — people in the most sophisticated cities of Europe and America and in isolated jungles of

Africa. It continues to speak to the hearts of people and point them to Jesus Christ, the only hope of our world. As you read this account of the world-wide impact of *JESUS*, your vision will be stretched and your burden increased for those who do not know of Christ. This film also will challenge you to live and witness for Christ where He has placed you.

— Billy Graham

INTRODUCTION

Settle in for an exciting reading treat. A special warning: You may not be able to put this book down, once you start reading. That was my experience. I thoroughly enjoyed this remarkable collection of stories of the miracles accompanying the development and worldwide showing of *JESUS*, the world's most translated film.

Thirty-eight years ago God gave me a vision to produce a film on the life of Christ. Since a majority of the world's population cannot read, a film seemed the best way to present Christ to the multitudes. On many occasions through the years the board of directors of Campus Crusade for Christ discussed the need for such a film. For me, the completion of this film, and its use by many mission organizations worldwide, is the fulfillment of that dream.

The response to *JESUS* has proved that it is one of the greatest evangelistic tools in history. Each night somewhere in the world many teams of workers are showing *JESUS* to several hundred thousand people in villages, rural areas and urban communities, and to high school and university students. Between 30,000 and 50,000 are indicating their desire to receive our Lord Jesus Christ each day.

When God gave me the vision of the film on the life of Jesus, I did not have the money to produce it. Nor did Cecil B. DeMille, whom I approached with my dream. Yet years later, in God's perfect timing, He sent along John Heyman, a well known Jewish movie producer with a burden to put the Bible on film and to tell the story of his Messiah. Dear friends of our ministry, Bunker and Caroline Hunt, also had caught the vision for worldwide evangelism, and they offered to underwrite the entire cost of production. In the meantime, the ministry of Campus Crusade for Christ had expanded into 150 countries, where we were helping train millions of Christians from thousands of churches of all denominations to share Christ. On campuses, thousands of committed young men and women were trained to carry the film into some of the world's most inaccessible places.

The coming together of these factors made the development and the incredibly rapid worldwide deployment of the *JESUS* film possible.

Maybe you have an unfulfilled dream or vision to do something significant for the Lord. You may have become discouraged and are about to abandon the vision God placed in your heart. If so, please do not give up. You can be sure that what God tells you to do, He will, in His appointed time, enable you to do. You simply need to trust God and obey His command (Philippians 2:13).

We've seen this happen with the *JESUS* film. More than thirty years passed after God gave the burden for a film on the life of His Son before all the various factors were right. Then in His sovereignty and wisdom, He provided the finances through Bunker and Caroline Hunt, and the technical expertise for producing the film in John Heyman. Then He had Paul Eshleman ready to orchestrate the development and distribution, along with tens of thousands of staff and volunteers around the world. Hundreds of millions of people have viewed this film of the greatest life ever lived, in a hundred different languages; and it is our prayer target to show the film to five billion people in 271 languages and 1,000 dialects by A.D. 2000.

I became acquainted with the writer of this book when he and his wife, Kathy, were directing a dynamic Campus Crusade for Christ ministry at the University of Wisconsin. Because of his spiritual leadership and developmental skills in management, we asked Paul to coordinate Explo '72, an unprecedented week-long student training event for 80,000. Soon after that I asked him to direct the Campus Ministry of Campus Crusade for Christ.

Paul brought the same godly faith and leadership he exhibited in his other assignments to the *JESUS* film production and distribution. Both Paul and I are grateful for the vast army of men and women God has raised up to show the *JESUS* film night after night around the world, often at the risk of their lives.

The stories of God's preparation of men and events in this book are evidence of a sovereign God honoring obedience to a vision. But they are also proof that God still moves in the hearts of men and women when they hear the greatest story ever told about the greatest life ever lived. It is the purpose of this book to give glory, praise and thanksgiving to God for all that He has done and is doing through the *JESUS* film.

For both Paul and me it is particularly gratifying to see the film *JESUS* used by many ministries concerned about evangelism in developing countries. As a movement we are committed to helping fulfill the Great Commission — and this book enables you to lift the curtain a little and see God at work all over the world accomplishing His holy purpose. We ask that as you read these stories you will prayerfully consider how you can become a partner in world evangelization, especially by helping us to expand the use of the *JESUS* film throughout the world.

Bill Bright

CHAPTER ONE
MASAILAND

Rivulets of perspiration trickled down my back as I picked my way along the unmarked path a few yards behind Steve Dudugjian. The blazing African sun had been beating down on us since early morning, but now, as it dipped lower in the wide, clear sky stretched across Southern Kenya, it was beginning to lose its fire. We had walked several miles from the Tanzanian border, working our way closer to the Masai "manyatta" (village) that was our goal.

My body ached and I was grateful when we reached the top of a rise and stopped to rest. As I took it all in, I was filled with a sense of excitement at God's creation. As far as I could see, thorn trees and jacaranda dotted the landscape. Thompson gazelle and wildebeest moved slowly in the afternoon sun, and Steve pointed out herds of impala, and what looked like handpainted black and white zebra.

Africa! Years ago I had asked God for adventure in my life, but I could not have dreamed what He held in store for me. Steve and I were here as part of a team taking the film *JESUS* to the Masai. An estimated four hundred thousand of these tall, ebony-skinned people wander the bush country of Tanzania and southern Kenya. They have herded their cattle for centuries in this area, grazing them where the grasses grow, moving on when the pasturelands run out. For fifty years missionary efforts among these cattle-herding nomads have produced little results and very few conversions, but times have changed, and Steve Dudugjian and others in the area have been encouraged by the response they are seeing to the message of Jesus.

Steve handed me a canteen. I swallowed the cold water gratefully and wiped my mouth on my shirt sleeve, leaving a thin trail of mud in the dust I had collected on the journey. "How did you end up here, Steve, in the middle of nowhere?"

An easy smile spread across his face. "I guess I'd have to say it started in Vietnam. The Marine scouting unit I was with was wiped out." He paused, remembering. "I was shot in the head, blinded, and left for dead, but when the helicopter rescue team finally came back to pick up our bodies, somebody discovered I was still breathing. I spent one long year in a hospital, and I figured God spared my life for a reason. I believe it was to help people — like the Masai — get to know Him better." He looked out across the valley. "I guess I'm just thankful for what God did for me."

Steve had recovered only 2% of his eyesight and would never see more than a tunnel-like image a quarter-inch across, yet being with him made me tend to forget he was so nearly sightless. He could manage every conceivable situation and was able to do almost everything unassisted except drive a car.

He ran his hand through his curly black hair and stood to his feet. Tired as we were, we would have to get back on the trail again if we were to reach the manyatta before nightfall. We had begun this leg of the journey the day before in the shadow of Mt. Kilimanjaro, in Namanga, a village on the Tanzanian border. It is a haven for smugglers, thieves and prostitutes, but we saw hundreds express a desire to receive Christ as they watched His life unfold on the screen. Late that night we stretched out on wooden benches in an abandoned church building. Exhausted, but deeply moved, I had finally drifted into a few hours of much-needed sleep. As we began walking again, I wondered whether Steve was as weary from our schedule as I was, but I was too busy trying to keep up with him to ask.

Not far from the path a giraffe craned his slender neck, plucking the choicest leaves from a rambling African thorn tree. I followed the wide path Steve made around a red mud anthill towering fifteen feet above our heads. "Steve," I asked, "how did you start with the Masai?"

"Through Mattayo."

"Who's that?"

"A former Masai warrior who's recently become a Christian," he said.

"How did he find Christ?"

"It's kind of a long story," Steve said, "but it used to be that a Masai boy became a warrior only if he could kill a lion with his spear. Kenya has since banned the hunting of lions, so manhood for the Masai is achieved in different ways now, but Mattayo killed his lion.

"Then a few months later he was with a friend on his lion hunt, when the animal turned on his friend, attacking him. Mattayo rushed the lion and killed it with his spear. Shaken and frightened, he returned to his injured friend. The boy lay bleeding in the dust, his stomach nearly torn out of him. Mattayo scooped him up in his arms and carried him about twenty kilometers to a mission station."

"What happened to the boy?"

"He died a few hours later," Steve said, "but Mattayo learned about Christ from the missionaries and decided to become a Christian. He returned to his tribe a great hero because of his lion killing — kind of the Roger Staubach of Masailand — until he told them he had become a Christian. Then everything changed. The other warriors forced him to fight them, and even though he defeated them all they stole his cattle and persecuted him and made his life unbearable.

"He left his manyatta, and we met him a few months later. With very little coaching he learned to share his faith, and for the last six or eight months he's been walking from one manyatta to the next, talking to his people about Jesus."

"Did he have anything to do with getting into the manyatta we're going to now?" I asked.

"It's a direct result of his witnessing. He's fearless! A few months ago he was talking to a witch doctor in a village near here when the witch doctor became very angry with him and tried to kick him out of the village. But Mattayo stood his ground telling the witch doctor that Jesus' power was stronger than any of his black magic. As he spoke, the witch doctor just dropped to the ground, trembling, and when he finally stood up he told Mattayo, 'You come back tomorrow. I want to talk to you.'

"Everyone was afraid the witch doctor would put a hex on Mattayo if he returned. They all knew it could cost him his life and urged him to leave while he could, but Mattayo said, 'If I die it will be for the Lord.'

"The next day when Mattayo returned to the witch doctor's hut he was surprised to find it full of people. They asked Mattayo to speak to them, so for more than an hour he told them about God's love and Jesus' death for their sins while the witch doctor stood silently in the back of the hut. Then slowly he stood and walked toward Mattayo while everyone watched in silence.

"'I will speak now,' the witch doctor said. He looked Mattayo in the eye then turned to the people and said, 'Yesterday when this man spoke about Jesus, something happened to me. It was as if a big cross came out of the sky, went down through my body and cleaned all the bad out of me. I must tell you I am now a follower of Jesus, and every one of you will be too.'" Steve glanced over his shoulder at me and grinned. "The witch doctor's hut is where the house church meets now."

"I love God's sense of humor!"

"Mattayo and I made a visit to this manyatta together several weeks ago. They told us it was the first time they had ever let a white man in. You have to remember, this is no ordinary village, Paul. It's their warrior initiation camp — the fiercest fighters of the Masai are there. It was a little tense at first, but we had a great time!"

A little tense at first. Knowing Steve Dudugjian that could mean a lot of things. I wondered about the reception we would receive when we got there, and I picked up my pace to close the distance between us. I breathed a prayer of thanks to God for yet another adventure! Looking back on the struggle I had put up, trying to keep God away from the controls of my life seemed so foolish now. But I had been convinced that committing my life to Christ would mean no more than being sentenced to a kind of gray boredom. I could not have been more wrong.

It wasn't until a close friend asked what I was going to do with my life that I really gave God much serious thought. I had just graduated from college and wanted to make some money and find some excitement! I was only fooling around with God . . . until someone who loved me looked me straight in the eye and asked, "When are you going to get off the fence?"

That night I could not get the question out of my mind. I tried ignoring it, but it would not be ignored. I tried reading and couldn't concentrate. Even television did nothing to take my mind off the gnawing struggle going on inside me. *What will you do with Jesus?*

There was sin in my life that I was not ready to confess. If the truth were known, I did not want to give it up. I lived like a Christian — most of the time — but I was not sure I really wanted to do what God might ask of me if I gave Him my life. *I* wanted to go into business; *I* wanted to make a lot of money; *I* wanted to feel that what I was doing was important; *I* had to have *a cause, a challenge, a purpose worth dying for.*

Around midnight that night, I opened my Bible to some familiar verses:

No soldier in active service entangles himself in the affairs of everyday life, so that he may please the one who enlisted him as a soldier (2 Timothy 2:4).

I was planning to get as entangled as I could in the business world.

But just as we have been approved by God to be entrusted with the Gospel, so we speak, not as pleasing men but God, who examines our hearts (1 Thessalonians 2:4).

As I stared into the blackness of my room I began to wonder about the condition of my heart. How hardened had I become to spiritual matters, to God's voice? I wrestled with my doubts and desires as surely as if they were flesh and blood. Would I hear His voice if He spoke to me again? If I did not turn and walk toward Him right now, would there be another time for me?

The battle raged within me for what seemed an eternity until, wet with sweat, I dropped to my knees beside my bed and cried out, "Father, I know You're in my life because I claimed You as a child, but I've been so rebellious. *I don't want to sit on the fence anymore.* Forgive me, and help me to turn from my sin. I want to be pure and holy before You." But I knew I was still holding back. It was so hard to let go . . . but I wanted to. "Lord," I prayed, "take over my life. I'll go *anywhere*, do *whatever* You want me to."

Quietly as I talked to God the crushing weight I was wrestling with slipped away and I found I could breathe again. I had counted the cost . . . and had given Him my pride. I crawled back into my bed and slipped off to sleep like a child who feels safe knowing his Father is there.

And now, only a few short years later, I found myself in Africa, with Steve Dudugjian, headed toward a Masai warrior initiation camp to share the gospel of Jesus Christ in the Masai language through the life-changing film *JESUS*. I never dreamed what freedom and excitement there would be in laying down my pride. And in return, God had given me what I longed for: life with a purpose. I was *living* the greatest adventure I could have imagined!

Suddenly, just ahead of me Steve stopped in his tracks. His body was tense and stiff. I looked up and could not believe my eyes. Wildly painted Masai warriors had appeared out of nowhere, and before we could move, we were surrounded by two dozen fierce-looking natives, each gripping a menacing, razor-sharp spear.

"Steve?"

"Stay calm," he said. "Just stay calm."

CHAPTER TWO
WARRIOR SPEARS

I swallowed hard, wishing my heart would beat quieter, slower, but I could not control the pounding in my chest. I was being sized up, or so I felt as I looked into the eyes of the men surrounding us. They talked among themselves, perhaps discussing what to do with us. I glanced at Steve, hoping he understood what they were saying, but he just shrugged, and said things would be all right once we were able to see the chief.

As I looked around me at the Masai, it was as if I had been transported into another space and time. Nothing had changed for these people in hundreds of years. Their faces were smeared with red ocher, and the spears they carried were the same as those their grandfathers used to kill lions and to dispose of enemies who invaded their territory. Their long black hair was plaited and covered with mud, and hand-carved sticks had been woven in at their foreheads and the backs of their necks. They covered their nakedness with faded, rough-textured blankets drawn around their shoulders. Several wore metal or wooden rings around their ankles and wrists, and their earlobes had been stretched until they hung in wide circles reaching almost to their shoulders.

They are a handsome people, tall and thin with delicate features and stately carriage. Spears, knives and all, these are people that Jesus loves, yet as I stood there, wondering what was going through their minds, I could not help but remember countless stories of missionaries who had died in circumstances like ours. Steve and I had no way to tell these people that their chief had asked us to come. We could only begin to walk slowly toward the manyatta and hope that they meant to do us no harm.

Within minutes we were standing at the edge of a circle of eighty or ninety huts. Dried thorn bushes had been piled high between them to protect the cattle in the center from wild animals. Steve and I were relieved to meet the chief, who explained to the others that we were friends. We were welcomed warmly, and then the excitement mounted as the jeep drove in carrying the film equipment and the rest of the team, including Jim Green, a veteran missionary to Africa.

We went to work, quickly setting up the portable screen and projector in the center of the circle of huts. The cattle wandered over, poking into the edges of our equipment as we hauled in the generator and pipes for the screen. We picked our way around as carefully as possible — the ground was covered with layers of cow dung. The Masai use it with sticks to build their huts, and while we worked, one weathered old woman slopped a load of fresh "building material" into the cracks in the roof of her hut. At the same time she was watching us with great curiousity.

Several hefty bulls with horns at least two feet long began cruising the area where I was struggling with the anchor ropes for the screen. The closer they got, the more concerned I became about the equipment . . . and my body. In my finest sign language, I gestured my concerns to a warrior standing nearby. He nodded, and I felt a little foolish when he sent a five-year- old boy with a stick to whack the biggest bull soundly on the nose.

Before long, everything was set up and running. The night was hot and still, not a breath of air stirring. In the flickering light of the projector I looked around me. Flies crawled across the upturned faces of the people but they seemed not to notice. They were drawn into the motion picture on the big white screen in the circle of cow dung huts. These backward people, frozen in time, unchanged in thousands of years, were watching the first film in history to be translated into the Masai language. For the first time in their lives they were hearing the message of God's love for them.

Unexpected tears blurred my vision as I reflected on what an incredible privilege was mine to be among the first in the world to bring the Good News of Jesus to these people who had *never heard*! What could compare with this? What better thing could I do with my life? In the days that would follow, many who would have died without Christ would turn to Him because we brought the message of salvation. What we were doing had an eternal purpose with eternal results. How I wished that every Christian could taste the excitement of sharing Christ on the "frontier," in the uttermost parts of the earth. Bored and blasé Christians would never feel the same about their faith again. It was an experience beyond words. It was intoxicating! And completely humbling.

And then I understood what C. T. Studd must have felt when he returned to his home in England hoping to recruit others to help in the pioneer mission venture he had begun in Africa. Christians were unmoved, uncaring,

and in response to their cold indifference he penned these
words:

> "Some may wish to live
> Within the sound of church and chapel bell;
> I want to run a rescue shop
> Within a yard of hell!"

There, in that unreached village of the Masai, we
were reaching people for Christ in a way that had never
before been done. We were going where they were, on
their terms, telling the Good News in their language. We
had opened a "rescue shop" for those who had never heard.

My thoughts were interrupted with the sputtering of
the projector. It sparked and then went dead. I looked
over at Jim Green and he smiled.

"You ready to preach?" he asked.

"You're not serious."

His smile broadened as he informed one of our interpreters that I was going to speak.

What would I talk about? I wondered during the
thirty-five seconds I had to prepare. *What do they know
about Jesus, and God? Probably nothing. The Bible?
They've never heard of it.*

And then I found myself standing with an interpreter
at my side while everyone waited. The giant African moon
bathed the hundred or so upturned Masai faces with a
gentle light, giving them a silvered beauty.

"I have come tonight to tell you about the greatest
God in the universe and His Son, Jesus. The God I speak
of created this world. He made the grass, the animals,
and all cattle. He is the most powerful Person in the

universe. He will live forever; He lives now in a great home beyond the sky, and He cares about you and me.

"Men have always wondered what God looked like. They wondered if He was a good spirit or an evil spirit. They wanted to know what God was like, but they did not know how to find Him.

"Until one day God decided to send His Son into the world to show men what the one, true, and most powerful God was like. The name of His Son is Jesus. The film we were showing you is about Jesus, God's Son. We will fix the machine and show you the story of His life another night.

"The Great God has said that only people who are perfect can live beyond the sky with Him forever. We are not perfect. We want things that belong to others. We steal cattle. We steal someone else's knife or spear. But Jesus can make it possible for us to be with God. Tomorrow we will explain how Jesus can get God to accept us even though we have done bad things."

It was a beginning, but I realized how much I took for granted. I saw too how the film explained it all so much quicker and clearer than I ever could.

One of the team members leaned up against a dung hut. "What happens now?" I asked him.

"Get some sleep," he said. "We'll go back to Nairobi in the morning for the equipment we need and try to make it back by dark. Then we'll try it again."

Jim Green and I decided to find our sleeping quarters but instead found ourselves in the grip of several strong hands. We turned to face three grinning warriors. *What's going on*? I wondered. Our interpreter must have read my mind, or maybe it was the panic in my eyes. "They want you to dance with them," he said. He smiled broadly and shooed us into the circle. "It's O.K. Go on. They're going to jump."

We picked our way between drowsy cattle, over to a clearing where several warriors were already dancing. Drums made from hollowed logs and stretched animal skins sang out a festive beat, and as Jim and I arrived, the few old women and the children of the village clasped hands and circled around, moving to the rhythm.

Inside the circle the men were jumping, and I was amazed at what I saw. With spears by their sides in one hand and small clubs in the other, these Masai were leaping two and a half or three feet into the air from a standstill.

"Can you imagine the kind of basketball players or high jumpers these guys would make?" I asked Jim. They were jumping all around us, and signaling us to join the dance. *Why not?*

I picked a spot in the circle and ventured my finest leap, but before I hit the ground the Masai were in stitches. They were laughing at *me.* Jim jumped and the warriors responded the same, enjoying whatever we were doing "wrong." Our competitive natures overruled our injured pride, and we both decided to figure out what was making them laugh.

For one thing, the Masai were all barefooted and Jim and I were jumping in hightop, laced boots, a major difference. But with two pounds of cow dung and mud clinging to the bottoms of our feet we decided the advantage was not important enough to take our shoes off for. Not here!

We continued to jump, and they continued to laugh. Then they began to mimic us and we could see that it was more than the boots. We had been throwing our hands in the air on every jump, which is great when going after a tip-off in basketball, but not for warriors armed with spears and clubs. A guy could get hurt that way.

The drumbeat changed and the pace became faster, the steps more syncopated. Jim and I tried but we could not keep up. Then the men moved out of the circle, choosing partners for this dance. There were no eligible young women permitted in this manyatta since sexual relations are forbidden during the seven long years of training, so they picked little six- and seven-year-old girls as their partners. The rhythm of the drums quickened again, and the movements became faster and sexually suggestive.

Jim and I dropped out and just watched what seemed to be some sort of mating dance. A warrior who was particularly pleased with a child might touch her shaved head with the tip of his hair, a sign of great favor since no one was permitted to touch the hair of a warrior until he had completed his initiation.

As the dancing continued a consciousness of how far we were from civilization sunk in a little deeper and I wondered what we would do if these men became offended over our not dancing. I scanned the faces watching the dancers, looking for our interpreter but he had vanished, and I wondered if we could find him if we needed to.

"Jim," I asked, "do you think we're in any danger here? I mean, they're not likely to get violent, are they?"

"I don't think so," he said. I had hoped for a somewhat more definite answer. "The Masai are among the fiercest warriors in Africa; the other tribes really fear them. In all the years I've lived in Nairobi I've never heard of a missionary being permitted in a warrior camp like we are tonight. There's really no precedent. No one's ever done it to my knowledge."

Somehow I was not comforted by Jim's words. "What do you say we head back?" I searched the long crescent of identical huts. "Hey Jim," I asked, "which hut are we supposed to sleep in?"

"There was a big white cow in front of it." He grinned at me. "If she's moved, we're in trouble."

Somehow we found the hut, which we fondly dubbed the "dungalow." A toothless, old-looking woman, who I guessed to be a grandmother, handed us each a lump of something she had cooked for us. It looked like cold, clumped Cream of Wheat, and she called it "ugali." She pointed to an iron pot simmering on a grate over the fire in the center of the hut. It was goat soup, or stew, and she motioned for us to dip our lumps of "mush" into it. We followed her directions, and found it only moderately terrible. We ate a lot, partly because we were hungry, partly because we did not want to upset her since we still had not found our interpreter. When our hostess looked away Jim whispered that I was holding my ugali in my "toilet hand" and I quickly switched, hoping that the lady of the hut had not already noticed my breach of manners.

After dinner we laid our dusty, tired bodies down on the cowskin mats our hostess pointed out. As I struggled with the laces on my boots she settled in a corner and began nursing a small child. These women's lives are so hard that most of them appear to be much older than they are.

The child finally fell asleep curled up on her pallet, and the woman left the hut, returning in a few minutes carrying a beat-up bucket half filled with dirty looking water.

As she began to wash herself Jim whispered, "You familiar with the custom of the Masai, Paul?"

"No."

"When they want you to know you are a friend, they give you their wife for the night," he said.

"Listen," I said, "if any favors are to be handed out, as the resident missionary I think you should be first in line. I'll just be over here under my sleeping bag."

I was joking, of course, but Jim wasn't. What if this woman came crawling over onto our cowskins wearing only a big smile? We would say no and curl up in our bags; she probably would not understand our moral code and would be offended. Then she would tell the warriors in charge, and before we could speak we could be in a lot of trouble. I thought of Jim Elliott, murdered by the Auca Indians while bringing them gifts because of Jesus' love.

I lay there, pretending to be asleep, with my hand loosely draped across my eyes. I squinted through my fingers, straining to see into the darkness until I decided that this Masai woman probably had such keen night vision she could see the whites of my eyes through my fingers. I was torn between faking sleep and trying to see what was going on. Curiosity can be a curse.

From her neck and long, dangling earlobes the woman removed several strands of colorful beads and trinkets and placed them in a tin box. She dipped a soiled piece of rag in the murky wash water beside her and sponged the dust and dirt from her face and arms. Then squatting on the dung floor, she picked up a little stick and scraped the manure and mud from her feet. Jim and I each breathed a silent sigh of relief when she wrapped herself in a coarse, red blanket and settled down on her cowskin to sleep.

But for Jim and me, sleep was elusive in our cramped quarters. The fire burned lower but the hut was still unbearably warm, and next to our bed in a pen made of sticks was the family's calf, asleep and the picture of peacefulness. Masai families house their small animals inside their huts to protect them from lions and other wild animals roaming the night.

I rolled onto my back and looked at Jim. He smiled wryly and shook his head. After two days in the bush I was sure our deodorants had failed miserably, but alongside the calf no one would have suspected.

I had finally drifted off to sleep when I heard shouting, and woke with a start to find three warriors crowding into the hut. My first thought was that Jim and I had wandered into the wrong place and were sleeping on their cowskins. But our hostess emerged from her blanket roll and rekindled the cook fire. I looked at my watch. It was 1:30 A.M. and dinner was about to be served.

As the warriors waited for their food, they sat by our feet playing with our flashlights and trying on our boots. They were amazed at the experience, and I was amazed that at twenty-five or thirty years of age they had never worn a pair of shoes. I was reminded again of where I was.

Sometime after 2 o'clock the men had enough to eat and left the "dungalow," and our hostess began her bathing ritual again. As I tried to sleep the thought crossed my mind that one of the warriors might have asked her whether she had "shown us a proper good time," and there might still be a chance that she would show up on one of our cowskins. But she dug the last of the manure from between her toes and rolled up in her blanket for the last time that night and everyone fell asleep; until the calf began bawling for his mother . . . at 5:30 in the morning.

CHAPTER THREE
AN
INCREDIBLE TOOL

We were not in Africa by accident. The remarkable film *JESUS* that we were using was not just a "lucky break" for the heathen in this particular area. What was happening here is Masailand was being repeated all over the world.

While we waited in the manyatta for the projector to be fixed, teams in 110 countries were showing the *JESUS* film, often to crowds in tribes that had never seen a film. In the mountains of Thailand a thousand Buddhists would see His story for the first time. Guerillas in El Salvador would hear the words of the Prince of Peace as they looked at the film on a dirty, white-washed wall. In the Middle East, Muslim oil sheiks would turn the sound low on their television sets as they watched the film in Arabic on smuggled black market cassettes.

And behind the entire project — from the production and the finance to the translation and distribution — was Campus Crusade for Christ. For the past 20 years I had been privileged to be a part of the staff — to work with mission pioneers like Jim Green, Steve Dudugjian and Don Myers. Now there were more than 16,000 co-workers

worldwide and their leadership would prove to be the key
to the rapid spread of the *JESUS* film.

This Masai village out here in the "bush" country
didn't really resemble a college campus, the original
evangelistic setting for Campus Crusade for Christ. But
then, Campus Crusade had grown beyond a ministry to
only students years ago. Its non-denominational nature
and its single-minded dedication to evangelism and discipleship had produced tremendous expansion. Now the
JESUS film was becoming the most effective evangelistic
and discipleship tool in the history of the movement.

In my earliest association with Crusade there had been
a slogan: "Win the campus for Christ today — win the
world tomorrow." I could see it happening — not just
through the Campus Crusade ministry, but everywhere.
Students from many different ministries were saying "forget
it" to the materialistic rat race, and committing their lives
to taking the message where nobody else had gone. In
the upcoming summer, thousands of students from scores
of organization and churches would be showing the *JESUS*
film everywhere from villages along the Amazon to the
refugee camps of Africa.

I thought about what a key tool for evangelism this
film had become remembering its origins. To Dr. Bill
Bright, the founder of Crusade, it clearly was especially
gratifying. It was the fulfillment of a life-long dream and
vision from God. During the months of production we
had talked about it often.

As a young Christian in 1947, God had given to Bill
a strong desire to produce a film on the life of Jesus that
could be used for worldwide evangelization. Living in
Hollywood at the time, he began to approach various
producers to discuss the project. Among those he met was

the great director Cecil B. DeMille, who had produced
the historic film on Jesus called *King of Kings*.

For lack of funds, the making of the film kept being
delayed. It was not yet God's timing. However, the burden
to produce the film on the life of Jesus continued to grow.
Year after year, board members of Campus Crusade for
Christ discussed the need for a film on the life of Jesus.
Yet more than thirty years would pass before God was
ready to make this vision — the vision he had placed in
Bill's heart — a reality.

Now the film had been translated into more than a
hundred languages and was being seen by hundreds of
thousands of people every night. Reports indicated that
10 to 20 percent of those who saw the film in various
areas were expressing interest in becoming followers of
Jesus. Not all areas were so receptive but there was interest
everywhere.

And beyond that, Campus Crusade had now made the
film available to over a hundred other mission organizations. This was a film that could help the entire body of
Christ. It needed to be shared.

For Bill Bright and the Campus Crusade ministry, this
trek to the Masai was simply a further unfolding of God's
plan to take His message to the ends of the earth. To the
Masai, however, the film was to become very important.

During our days in this initiation camp, the faith of
Chief Ole Michiri was strengthened. He had become a
believer in Jesus just a short time before through the
tireless, loving concern of Mattayo.

What none of us knew, was that Michiri was to become
chief of all the warriors of Kenya and Tanzania at the
next initiation ceremonies. He could open the way for the
whole tribe to see *JESUS*. But it could be dangerous.

A silent watchfulness pulsed through the warm African air that first night in camp. This manyatta (village) had been erected for two weeks of celebration and ceremonies marking the end of seven long, hard years of intensive training for more than two thousand Masai men. They had made it! They would return to their manyattas as respected warriors, but first they would be coming here from their training camps all around Kenya and Tanzania to go through the long-awaited initiation ceremonies, and to celebrate with no holds barred. They had earned a good time!

Quarters at the "Masai Hilton" were less than elegant, consisting of a wide circle of some four hundred huts made of sticks and cow dung. The spaces between the huts had been filled with limbs of African thorn trees to discourage lions and other wild animals from prowling the camp during the night and devouring cattle...or neighbors.

It was late afternoon when the *JESUS* film team arrived at the entrance to the manyatta. Steve Dudugian stepped out of the jeep to greet the chief of the combined tribes, Ole Michiri. The smiling Armenian missionary held out his hand in friendship to the lean, aristocratic Masai chief. Michiri could not seem to talk fast enough of his plans for the *JESUS* film.

"I want you to show it tonight and tomorrow night, before the ceremonies begin," he said. "Then, as the others come to join us in the camp, you will show it every night for all of them, each of the five nights during the ceremonies. They must all see the film! They must all know Jesus!"

Ole Michiri's enthusiasm was contagious. Excitement danced in his eyes as he spoke of his plan to share the

Jesus he loved with his people. Nothing mattered more to him than spreading the Good News to his brothers.

It was an exciting honor for the film team to be in the warrior manyatta at this special time for them. Outsiders had never been invited to share in these private and sacred ceremonies. Seasoned missionaries who had spent most of their lives among the Masai called this a once-in-a-lifetime opportunity, but they warned against the dangers.

Four of our film team members were former warriors themselves. Before becoming Christians they had gone through an initiation like the one being prepared for now, and they wrestled with feelings of apprehension about the next few days.

During the ceremonies a great bull would be sacrificed and the warriors would share a potion of blood, milk and urine as part of their initiation as elders of their tribes. Now they would shave their long, plaited, mud-covered hair for the first time, and revoke all the restrictions they had been living under. They would dance, and celebrate, and fill themselves with home-brewed whiskey every day. And no one would stand in their way. Anything could happen.

At the entrance to the manyatta, several Masai were already brewing an ample supply of soon-to-be whiskey. (Beside them an enterprising Masai from the city had built a small shack and was selling soda, tea and bottled beer.)

What kind of reception would *JESUS* receive? Was this the right time? Ole Michiri insisted there would never be a better time. For some of those who would come to this manyatta in the next few days, it might be the *only* time they would hear the gospel.

That first night they set up the screen and equipment, and strung a lengthy light cord between two thorn trees.

The cord was fixed with light bulbs every ten to fifteen feet. When darkness covered the village, they started the projector, and soon several hundred warriors gathered around to watch the picture, most of whom had never seen a film. At the end of the showing, one of our Masai team members stood beneath the unlit cord of lights and invited anyone who would like to know more about the Jesus of the film to "come to the light."

At those words another team member threw a switch and the lights over the speaker's head lit up brightly. The warriors jumped to their feet in surprise and ran toward the lights, touching them and talking excitedly. It was the first time most of them had seen a light bulb. When the excitement ebbed a little, the curious wandered away into the darkness, but seventy-five men stayed — interested in this man Jesus.

During the day team members visited the huts. At night we showed the film, and each time more Masai came to the light afterward to ask questions and to pray the prayer of invitation to Christ.

Every day the population of the village grew larger and louder. There were more than two thousand warriors by the fourth night, plus many women and small children, living in the manyatta. The dancing and drinking continued night and day with the atmosphere rowdy and wild. Everyone on the team felt tense and apprehensive.

Several hundred new warriors had arrived that day at the manyatta but had refused to join in with the others. They stayed separated, kept to themselves, stood on the outer edges of the circle, watching the dancing and festivities from a distance.

As darkness approached, the tension mounted and Steve called the team together for a time of prayer. One by one each member thanked God for giving them this rare opportunity and for what He planned to do. While they prayed, the fervor of the warriors' dancing climbed to a fever pitch as they jumped and whirled around the leaping flames of the bonfire.

Steve walked through the clearing toward the projector. No one would come tonight to see the film, but they would show it just the same. Ole Michiri had asked them to. The music of the sound track poured from the speakers as the film began and the team joined Steve in the empty clearing. Before long, though, they discovered they were not alone. The Masai were being drawn to the message. A few at a time left the dancing and drinking to sit quietly at the feet of *JESUS,* until two thousand ocher-painted warriors, plus elders and chiefs, women and children, had come to watch the film.

That night at the close of the film, team member Joseph Kihoro asked how many would like to invite Jesus Christ into their lives. Nearly 90 percent responded.

Today the Masai continue to respond to the gospel and many home churches have been started. They do not erect church buildings because they are a nomadic people, but it is not unusual to pass by a tall African thorn tree in the plains near the Tanzania border and find a growing congregation gathered underneath, worshiping together.

* * *

Missionary/writer Don Richardson has said that every people has a "redemptive analogy," which is a part of their culture and accepted custom, and through which they can receive forgiveness. The pastor of a thorn-tree church about four hours drive from Nairobi shared with me a most remarkable story about the Masai concept of sin and forgiveness.

It was spring in Africa, spring of the year of forgiveness. The witch doctor made his preparations and as he laid by the few things he would need for his journey, his heart was heavy. He was an old man. The task had fallen to him before, and yet he never had gotten used to it: the pain, the fear, the unfairness to the one who would be chosen, and to his family. He straightened his aging shoulders. He would do what he had to do. The price must be paid for this generation.

He traveled many miles on foot to a manyatta far from his own. There he met with the medicine man of that Masai tribe and together they fell on their faces and prayed earnestly to Satan. For hours they prayed, seeking what the old witch doctor had come for. And then it came.

Although the two men never had met before, and despite the fact that the younger man had not ever been away from his own manyatta, he said the names of four men who lived in the older man's village. The names had come from the heart of Satan.

The old man returned the long distance across the plains, his heart heavier with every step. Who would he tell first? How would they react? When would the tears stop? He knew each of the men, so young, so eager to live. Each had a family. Each had dreams. He had heard them laugh, had watched them hold their babies, had seen how brave they were in danger. What he had to do would change their lives: for one of the men, *forever*!

The children saw him first as he walked slowly across the plain to the manyatta. The blanket he wore blew against him in the wind, and he leaned a little heavier on the spear he carried in his trembling hand.

By the time he reached the small circle of cow-dung huts, the whole village had gathered to hear the names of those who had been chosen. They stood now in silence, watching him, each of them praying he would not say their name or that of one they loved. He looked into the faces of his people. He had advised them all his life — some of them, all of theirs. Then he drew a breath, and in a strong voice called out the four names he had been given, one after another until they all knew.

Mournful, pain-filled cries began as the families of these men let their grief spill out. No! It cannot be my husband, my father, my son! It must be someone else. Perhaps you heard the wrong name. Could you have heard the wrong name? *Please don't let it be him.*

Preparations were begun, but it seemed wrong somehow that a feast was being planned. Four families carried with them the burning fear that of the men named, it could be *their* husband, or son, or father who would be the price. It could be *the one they loved* who would live as an outcast, paying for the sins of his generation with the rest of his life. The price of redemption was too high.

The day arrived and the ceremony began that would point to the man who would be the "scapegoat" for the manyatta. The people of the village encircled the witch doctor and the four men. Rhythmically they swayed back and forth, waiting . . . waiting. Kneeling on the hardened ground in the center of the men, the old witch doctor raised his hand above his head and cast several small, marked pebbles at the feet of each man in turn. And then it was done. One had been chosen with the casting of lots. All were redeemed at the price of this one.

The scapegoat stood silently, his arms at his sides as the people moved away, away to celebrate the forgiveness of their sins, the return of the three men who were not chosen.

He looked into the eyes of his wife. His heart longed to hold her to him just one last time, but it could not be done. He was never to feel the touch of a human hand again. Anyone who touched an outcast would die.

His children wept as if their hearts were broken. His mother and wife embraced and together wailed their agony of loss. But it was his father he would never forget as he watched the old man he revered slowly turn away from him. For a brief moment he had held his gaze — then it was gone, and he knew the old man would not look on the son of his shame again.

Quickly, too quickly, the hut his family was allowed to build for him outside the village was finished, and he sat alone on the hard ground, watching them walk back to the manyatta he would never enter again. They would bring him food to eat and water to drink so that he could live, but there was nothing left to live for, not for the outcast who had given his life to pay for the sins of his people.

The native pastor smiled a broad, satisfied smile at me. "You know," he said, "one of the sweetest things I have ever done is to tell an outcast about Jesus. I cannot tell you the joy that comes over these men when they learn that the Savior has been the scapegoat for all mankind, that the sins of all generations have been paid for already by a man called Jesus."

CHAPTER FOUR
STRUGGLE
TO FAITH

Thousands of miles from the Masai, years before there was a film called *JESUS*, John Heyman sat in the plush office that reflected his success as a Hollywood producer. He stared at the contracts on his desk. The words — like the rest of his life — were a confusing blur. There had to be something more to life than the endless rounds of negotiating with cynical studio heads, the hours and hours of precious time spent placating spoiled actors, the unrelenting pressures to bring pictures in on budget. And for what?

He was not sure why, but something told him he might know where to find the answers he sought. He closed the door of his office and opened a Bible.

John had been raised in Europe by Jewish parents but never had read the Scripture for himself. Now he began to spend hours every day in it. The more he read, the more he came to believe that the Bible was the source of our roots, our heritage. It was the foundation of law, health, education and justice.

As his study continued a new dream began unfolding in his heart and soon John was back in production — this time to produce the entire Bible on film. It was a massive undertaking. John had financed some of Hollywood's biggest hits, films like *Chinatown, Grease,* and *Saturday Night Fever.*

Now he began to record the book of Genesis on film, working carefully, staying true to the scriptural account to the smallest detail. Within a year he had completed the first twenty-two chapters of Genesis. His dream was beginning to take shape. But as he began production on Luke's Gospel, he was forced to face the truth: Unless he located financial backing from somewhere, he was going to have to quit. Perhaps the American churches could catch the dream and would be able to help. It was worth a try.

* * *

It was 1976. In the San Bernardino mountains of California in a cabin near Lake Arrowhead, several of us involved in the national leadership of Campus Crusade for Christ had gathered for a day of prayer.

I Found It — New Life in Christ was under way all across the United States, but in some cities this enormous evangelistic media campaign was in serious trouble and in danger of collapse. There were too few workers to follow up those who called in for counsel, several television stations had declined to carry our spot announcements, and we were running out of money. The obstacles seemed endless.

We had set aside the entire day for prayer, but in the middle of the morning we received a call. The voice on the phone said Bill Bright, president of Campus Crusade, wanted us to take time out to meet a man who had some Bible films.

"I'm sorry," I said, "but we just do not have the time to see him today. We're in the middle of a crisis. Maybe some other time." And I hung up.

A few short minutes later the phone rang again and the same voice said simply, "Dr. Bright wants you to see this man *now*. He'll be there within the hour." And *he* hung up.

In less than an hour I heard a knock at the cabin door. The tall, slender man standing on the porch was loaded down with projector, films and cords. I took an armload of film canisters from him and he stuck out his hand.

"I'm John Heyman," he said. "Thank you for taking the time. I know you're busy."

"We are." I grasped his outstretched hand. "We'll have to limit you to thirty minutes, John. I hope you'll understand. Especially after the long drive up here."

He set to work threading the projector, explaining briefly his credentials and what we were about to see. John hoped that we would be willing to help him reach some of the 50,000 churches Campus Crusade was in touch with in America.

I listened to his presentation, but as hard as I tried I could not get my internal clock to slow down. It ticked impatiently as John spoke. Why now? Why today when we had so much to do? It was so important that we use the day wisely. Reluctantly I drew the shades and found a seat toward the back of the room.

But as we sat together in the half-darkened cabin, something happened. I found myself drawn into what I was seeing on the screen — and I forgot all about being impatient. The simple but dramatic portrayal of Creation was refreshing and wonderful.

The time had been used well. Everyone in the room sensed that something special had taken place.

Two weeks later I walked into a small coffee shop in San Bernardino where John waited in a booth near the back. I glanced around at the brown tile flooring, the worn red vinyl booths and counter stools. On each table was a half-full bottle of catsup, a jar of mustard and a two-slice toaster. The place must have been comic relief compared to the elegant dining establishments this Hollywood movie producer was used to. But John did not seem to notice.

The waitress brought our order and John began to talk. "I've been thinking about this meeting since we talked and I have two questions to ask. But you need to know more about me before you answer so let me fill you in a little on my background.

"I am a Jew. I was born in Germany, where my father was a broadcaster for the German national radio. As Hitler began to rise to power Father seemed to know what lay ahead. He shipped my mother, sister and me off to England and later escaped himself on a bicycle just one week before Hitler took over.

"The next few years were filled with pain and fear for all of us. It seemed that every day we received a letter that made my mother cry — news that another relative had died in Hitler's gas chambers or in some other hideous way in a concentration camp.

"The greatest liberal minds of that era came regularly to our home to meet with my father — people like Huxley and other members of the Fabian Socialist Society. I was exposed to philosophy — early and steadily — but somehow God was not spoken of, even through my father's illness and death. I feel that I know very little of God.

"That brings me to the questions I want to ask." He set his coffee mug back on the table. "How did you become a Christian, and why did you do it?"

John's eyes were intense as he listened with careful attention to what I said. I shared the Four Spiritual Laws with him and he asked deep and reflective questions.

"John," I asked, "would you like to invite Christ to come into your life?"

"Of course," he said. "Who wouldn't? But I can't. It would be like turning my back on six million Jews who died in the holocaust; I'd be a traitor to my heritage. Besides, I just don't think I could take the leap of faith you did."

We paid our bill and walked around the block, discussing the obstacles John felt stood between him and a decision for Christ.

In the parking lot he gave me a bear hug, and as we parted we both choked back tears.

There were long meetings and telephone conversations from various places around the world throughout the next six months. John was still searching. I mailed him things to read. Bill Bright answered questions as they met on several occasions. Then in March of 1977, I heard the words I had longed so to hear from my friend. John Heyman had received the Lord into his life.

CHAPTER FIVE
SERIOUS SHOW BIZ

In the providence of God, He brings men and organizations together to accomplish the goals and visions that He gives to them. But where does a film that becomes a tool to unleash God's miracle-working power come from? As with any birth, the *JESUS* film was not brought to life without pain, struggles and a few nervous moments.

Dr. Bright, ever a catalyst in evangelistic effort, was eager to assist any endeavor that would bring his years-long vision of a film on Christ's life to fruition. I was placed on special assignment with John Heyman's production company in New York, and plans were launched for the production of a two-hour, full-length motion picture. But financing would be the key. Since the Campus Crusade ministry was not in a position to underwrite the entire film, perhaps some of the major studios would get involved. There was a lot of work to be done.

The first question was story line. Should we simply choose one of the gospels to portray? If so, which one? Matthew presents Jesus as the King, Mark as the Servant, Luke as the Son of Man, and John shows Him as the

Son of God. We considered compiling all four accounts but that meant we would have a ten-hour movie on our hands, and who is wise enough to weigh the value of one segment of Scripture against another to decide what to leave out? We sought the counsel of religious leaders around the world and the unanimous recommendation was that we use Luke's account because of its completeness.

Deciding how to tell the story of Jesus was a key question. Since this film was to be as authentic as possible, shooting was to be done on location in the places where the events originally took place, or as close as we could get.

Bernard Fishbein prepared a screenplay from Luke's Gospel. There was no fooling around with the text, no invented dialogue. Every word that Jesus would speak would come from the Scriptures.

Within a month we sent the completed script to more than 450 religious leaders and scholars asking for their input. Their response was positive and enthusiastic, with several providing excellent suggestions that improved the screenplay.

Co-producer Richard Dalton began working on the cross-plot, calculating production costs for the film. His final projections came to nearly six million dollars for production, another three or four million would be needed for distribution.

Assistant producers Omri Maron and Mati Raz immediately immersed themselves in the process of locating just the right people for the parts in Israel. They spent long hours poring over the biographies and photographs of actors in Israel. Auditions were held in London and Tel Aviv. Key questions included: Who would play the part of Jesus? What would Peter look like? What kind of voice should he have?

We began plans for distribution in the United States, trusting that the production funds would soon be available. Key religious leaders were contacted.

Marc Tannenbaum, head of the American Conference of Christians and Jews, bestowed his blessing and backing.

"My primary concern," he said, "is that we don't add to existing anti-semitism by portraying the Jews as Christ-killers again."

That thought had never crossed my mind before; the Jews had not killed Christ. It was my sin that kept Him on that cross. It was true that the Jews were the ones who asked Pilate to crucify Jesus, but it was a Roman prosecutor who sentenced Him, and Roman soldiers nailed Him to the cross. It was the world that crucified the Savior. But we decided that to help prevent the Jews from being blamed for Christ's death we would introduce Pilate with the following words: "He was handed over to Pontius Pilate, the most vicious of all Roman procurators, alone responsible for the crucifixion of thousands." Marc showed his appreciation for our efforts and gave his endorsement to the film.

Archbishop Fulton J. Sheen personally gave us his warm approval.

"You have taken no liberty with the Gospel text," he stated, "and have surrounded the figure of Christ with either credible or authentic characters who blend into the history. You have produced a masterpiece. Not only will all Christian churches support a masterpiece of this kind, but so will all who love history and the portrayal of a life that has affected millions."

But everything hinged on finding the necessary finances for production. After weeks of contacting studios back in

Hollywood, New York, and London we were nowhere. Every door we pushed in trying to raise the production funds was closed and barred. Without the money the film would never become a reality. There seemed only one remaining possibility.

Campus Crusade for Christ had scheduled several weekend meetings designed to raise funds for world evangelism. John and I were scheduled to lead a special seminar on the first weekend. The topic: how a film on the life of Christ could be used to help reach the world. John also had been asked to talk of his faith at the dinner that Saturday night. Perhaps when they heard of the need, someone's heart would be stirred to back the project financially. We prayed, expecting the Lord to do great things.

Only a handful of people attended our seminar, including one man who monopolized the time arguing his personal views against any man portraying the Son of God on film. A gray pallor of discouragement settled in again.

"Maybe someone will see the need tonight," I said to John as we left the seminar. "At least you can tell them about it in your talk."

John spoke to a large and attentive audience that night. In just a few words, looking beyond his own discouragement, he opened up to them and revealed his love and his heart for the God of Abraham, Isaac and Jacob . . . the God John Heyman had learned to love and lived to serve. Many in the room wept openly as they stood up to applaud the soft-spoken man before them.

In a corner of the room, Caroline Hunt, touched deeply by John's words and spirit, shared her feelings with her husband, Bunker. That night they talked for several hours with Dr. Bright. By morning Bunker and Caroline Hunt had made the decision to underwrite the film. John and I drove down the mountain with a three-million-dollar guarantee and a dream that would become reality because one couple was committed to world evangelism enough to fund a movie, *JESUS*.

There are thousands of people throughout the world who want to make films with a Christian message. There are, however, few people willing to take the financial risks. It would be the faith and generosity of Bunker and Caroline, and other supporters of Campus Crusade for Christ, that would make this film on Christ's life available to millions.

* * *

With the funding secured, preparations in Israel began to move ahead rapidly. Some of the scenes called for at least two thousand bearded men. It would take an army of makeup personnel to glue beards on all those chins. So assistant producer Omri Maron persuaded some of the rural Jews in small villages to begin growing their own beards.

Art director Ray Stannard moved into the old fairgrounds in Tel Aviv and created a gigantic prop factory. Architectural drawings were made of every set and prop to be used in the film; each scene was planned down to the finest detail. Thirty carpenters, plasterers, painters and riggers made up the crew that began constructing the huge temple set.

Thousands of costumes, hats and turbans would be required, and Rochelle Zaltman spent days at the universities in Jerusalem researching the clothing in use at the time of Christ. To assure authenticity, it was decided that only hand-woven cloth would be used and it would be dyed in just the thirty-five colors known to be used then.

Once the construction of the garments had begun, every newly tailored article of clothing had to be "aged." Headbands had to show dirty perspiration stains, beggars' robes needed to look worn and tattered, and the dust from the roads was to cling to the hems of long garments.

The filming began. As the weeks went by, members of the crew, grizzled veterans of many location shoots, commented on how difficult the making of this film was. Perhaps it was the striving for accuracy and authenticity. Perhaps the forces of darkness would rather it not be made. In any case, the problems were numerous.

Brian Deacon, the actor portraying Jesus, caught pneumonia during the filming of the baptism scene when the dove wouldn't land on his shoulder. He stood in freezing water up to his waist for two hours while men on ladders threw birds at him. Birdseed was tried on his shoulders, but the doves either landed on his head or faced away from the camera. Two doves drowned and an hour and a half of film was used before one stalwart performer landed on his shoulder.

The goats kicked down the fences of the corral, and the sheep, donkeys, horses, dogs and chickens scattered all over the village. One of the donkeys threw himself off a cliff and committed suicide.

Finding people to participate in a movie is usually an easy job, but we were looking for faces of 2,000 years ago, faces like Christ saw when He was here. Zeev Zeigler, the extras manager, did a fantastic job. He drove around the Israeli countryside looking for Yemenites and Moroccans, whose physical characteristics have changed very little over the centuries.

Zeev found the people he wanted, but they were very primitive by modern standards. Some had never even seen a movie. They were not used to the concept of organized labor, and disliked it a great deal when they had to be on the job at 5:30 in the morning. They were not used to taking orders, in particular from an outsider, so Zeev appointed one or two organizers in each village to explain to the people what he wanted them to do and what was happening. By the time the filming was completed Zeev's extras had worked more than 160,000 "extra days."

Bob Lawrence, the make-up director, proved especially creative in the scene where Peter cuts off the ear of the high priest's servant. In preparing for the scene, he covered the actor's hair with something like a bathing cap. Then he painted what looked like the remains of the severed ear on the side. He attached an artificial ear and inserted a thin tube under the cap, connected to a small squeeze bottle of red liquid. He finished by putting a full wig and beard on the actor to cover the cap and tubing, and attaching a piece of nylon fishing line to the fake ear.

When the scene was filmed, Peter lunged at the servant, slicing the air with his knife. At that exact second someone off-camera pulled on the fishline and the actor squeezed the bottle hidden in his hand. The ear dropped to the ground and a convincing red liquid poured from the side of his head. A lot of work for a two-second scene, but very effective.

* * *

John had been hard at it for hours one day when my wife Kathy and I arrived at the fairgrounds in Israel. We could not help being touched by the magic of movie-making as we made our way toward the set where the day's filming was going on. Carpenters and other artisans walked scaffolds above us creating antiquity as we watched. We saw two-thousand-year-old houses where little Jewish children should have peered at us from the windows, hand-carved chariots that could have carried soldiers thundering through the streets of Rome. We were surrounded by "the past"; only the smell of new wood and fresh paint told the real story.

Blueprints tacked to slant boards at each set outlined every line and detail that would eventually appear on the screen, and all had been researched and documented. Over a five-year period of time, directing twenty-five people, Michael Manuel, head of the research department for the Genesis Project, had produced a 318-page document describing the life and times of Jesus.

From those pages, a production document had been assembled giving biblical, theological, historical, sociological, archaeological and geographical background for every one of the 1,028 scenes in the film.

Kathy and I found John busy with the scene in the temple courtyard where Jesus expelled the moneychangers. To our untrained eyes it seemed that bedlam prevailed. Lighting technicians scrambled around the catwalks and scaffolding, adjusting powerful floodlights and spotlights on stand-ins and extras until the effect was what the director wanted. Several hundred costumed extras milled around nearby, waiting in boredom to be called for the scene.

We walked the temple set with John as he made one last check of details, looking for any minute oversight that might detract from the authenticity of the film. He glanced at an oil lamp mounted on the stone wall by the gates and stopped.

"Omri," he shouted above the noise. From somewhere in the crowd the assistant director appeared at his side. "Where's the soot on the wall behind that lamp? It can't have burned there a hundred years and not left some soot behind." Omri quickly dispatched a workman, who clambered up a ladder and sprayed a hundred years of soot behind the lamp.

Places were called as an actor in beggar's clothing jogged past us headed toward his mark.

"Hey there," John called after him, "get rid of the Nikes!" Beneath the hem of his tattered tunic the actor wore a pair of bright green running shoes.

It was not uncommon to spot a Pharisee or Galilean in the crowd wearing a shiny wristwatch. At one point in the filming John's keen eye for detail led him to stop the cameras to smooth over the ripple-soled print of a tennis shoe in the dust.

* * *

In some ways it seemed strange to film a picture about the Son of God using so many nonbelievers. Yet as the weeks progressed, it became clear that even this was a part of the bigger plan. As usual, God knew what He was about.

Just after my arrival in Israel, assistant director Ted Morley approached me and asked if I could talk to the "disciples."

"They all want to know how they should play their parts," he said, "and since you know the Bible we thought you might know what to tell them. The truth is, most of them don't have a single line to speak, but they want to do it right, the way the disciples would have."

I was a little surprised at the request. They were actors, Jewish actors for the most part, and I suppose I expected their attitude toward all of this might be "just another job." But when I talked with them. I discovered quite the opposite.

These men had an attitude of reverence toward the picture and their part in it. I sensed they held a deep respect for the message of the film, almost as if they had been called to do a sacred task.

I watched with fascination as each new day of filming unfolded more of the gospel to them. These men were slowly coming to understand who this man, Jesus, really was. It was easy to see that the Holy Spirit was at work on the set, touching hearts, changing lives.

CHAPTER SIX
IS JESUS
A CHRISTIAN?

Mark stumbled across our company almost four months after we started shooting the film. He was a college drop-out, wandering around Europe hoping to "find himself" somewhere along the way, and he came to us looking for a job. We hired him to carry props on our second unit.

The third day on the job, Mark decided he would like to read the script for the film, and so that night before bed he pulled a Gideon Bible from the beat-up dresser in the hotel where he was staying in Tel Aviv. He began reading the Gospel of St. Luke and did not put it down until he had read the entire book. As he closed that Bible, he opened his heart to the God he had found within its pages.

By the end of the week we were shooting scenes from the resurrection and needed someone to play "the body." Mark volunteered. We drove to an empty field not far from where David had killed Goliath and began setting up to film the scenes in the tomb. I wondered where the tomb was until one of the location scouts pulled away several small bushes and revealed a cave-like opening into the ground.

Mark was sent to wardrobe while the rest of the crew set up. Cable-layers with flashlights pulled snake-like electric cords across the field and disappeared into the dark hole. Generators were cranked up and electricians followed with lights of all sizes to illuminate the cave. It was a limestone tomb carved into the ground, much like the one that Joseph of Arimathea had prepared for himself during the first century.

Quickly the cables were buried out of sight, footprints smoothed away and rehearsals called. Eight times Joseph's servant carried the body down the steep descent into the cave. Rehearsals done, it was time to film.

Cameras rolled and Joseph's servant came into view carrying the body just as they had rehearsed. He began the descent down into the tomb but having done it so many times already he found his arms more tired than he realized, and just as he reached the entrance he dropped the body on its head. Mark groaned with pain from under the blanket but assured us he was all right. We started over from the top.

After five takes and several hours we had what we wanted, and the body seemed none the worse for wear. What no one knew was that during that scene something had happened to the body that would change his life forever. Months later I received a letter from Mark:

  I don't know whether you remember me but I was the one who played "the body" the day we shot the resurrection scenes. That was a tough day for me — wrapped in a hot, itchy, woolen blanket for three hours. If you remember, I was dropped and pushed around most of the day.

  But while I lay on that slab of stone inside the tomb, it was as if God spoke to me. "Mark," He said, "I want

you to share My message with others." I just wanted you
to know I am writing you from Dallas Bible College. I
am studying to be a minister.

* * *

Mark had come to us in the midst of a personal
journey, deeply longing to "find himself," and God had
led him to the answers he had only hoped existed. What
better place in the world to find God than here in the
land the rest of the world calls holy? In my mind, this
should be where people would embrace God with open
arms; here at the origin of the roots of God's chosen people;
in the country where you can stand in the footprints of
the saints, see the places spoken of in the Old and New
Testaments alike, touch your foot where Abraham, Isaac,
and Jacob walked with God. But I quickly learned that
most of the people in this part of the world did not share
my somewhat romantic view.

One early morning on location I got into a conversation
with the sister of a Jewish member of the crew. We had
not talked long before our discussion turned to things of
God, and then to whether or not He existed.

"It must be wonderful to believe there is someone
who really cares what happens to us," she said. Her voice
was sad, wistful.

"It only takes faith," I said, "believing that God is
who He says He is."

"I suppose." She paused. "I guess I've been through
too much to believe anything anymore. Too many of my
relatives were killed in the Holocaust . . . " Her voice
trailed off.

"Faith is a simple act of the will," I said, "a decision
to trust God in spite of everything else around us."

The tears in her deep brown eyes spilled onto her cheeks and she quickly brushed them away. "You'll never know how much I would like to believe," she said, "but I can't. I just can't." And she walked away, longing for what was hers already. I sighed, and whispered a prayer that the Holy Spirit would help her see the truth she could not see.

* * *

Lunch beneath a canvas awning was a welcome break from the scorching sun. A light breeze teased at our paper napkins and cooled our sticky bodies as the twelve "disciples" and I sat around a table exploring the spiritual impact the film was having on their lives.

Nikko Mitai, who played Peter, was the first to speak. "Before I came to do this picture I didn't believe in God." He munched thoughtfully on his sandwich. "Now," he said, cautiously choosing his words, "now I believe in God, and I am thinking a great deal about Jesus." He flashed a disarming smile. "I like Jesus. I like Him very much."

"How about you, Simon?" I asked the disciple on Peter's left. "Has the film affected your faith in any way?"

Leonard Weinstein, a large man with a wide forehead and open face, played Simon, the son of Alpheus. He spoke with a thick accent different from the others'.

"I come from Russia," he said, "Leningrad. So this is all new for me."

"Why are you in Israel?"

"I wanted to get away from the communists. And I thought that since I am Jewish, maybe Israel is where I could go. But for three generations my family has not been believing in God." He looked me straight in the eyes. "Now," he said, "I would have to say I believe. I believe in God."

It was becoming more and more clear. These men were on set every day, eight and ten hours at a time, listening to words straight from Scripture, and God has promised that His Word will not return void. It was exciting to know that those involved in this film were being confronted with the gospel.

Not everyone wanted to move closer to God because of it — the man who played James treated the script as if it were just another story. But the actor who played Philip, and several of the others were so eager for answers that they shot questions at me for the rest of lunch. I could feel within them a respect and a kind of wonder over this film.

As I watched the disciples walk back into the sunshine and take their places with Jesus in the next scene, I felt a calm confidence that they were truly in God's hand. I did not need to press for a "decision," I was simply a part in the planting and tending of the harvest. God had assigned others in strategic places who were carrying the Word faithfully, and someday — when the fruit was ripe — the harvest would be brought to the granary.

* * *

Brian Deacon had been selected to play the part of Christ because he so effortlessly portrayed Jesus on the screen. His mannerisms and delivery were excellent, his speech impeccable, and since the filming had begun his dedication and hard work had been amazing. By 5 A.M. every morning he was in makeup, and on the set from 6:30 till the last rays of sunlight were gone. Around 9 P.M. he might be ready to "relax" a little, but that was when he began memorizing lines for the next day. Six days a week this was his schedule.

As I talked with the actor one evening over dinner I asked him, "Who is Jesus to you, Brian?"

"I have had a number of good conversations about that with Tom Panella, my stand-in," he said. "I was raised in a home in Oxfordshire. My mother was Catholic and my father Protestant, but they agreed that I should seek my faith for myself. Because of this I've probably spent more time than the average person evaluating what I believe. I believe that God sent Jesus to die for our sins; He is the Savior. But I don't know if I'll ever be like the Christians you have in America who go around saying they are 'born again.'

"The more I learn about Jesus the less sure I am that I will ever deserve to be called by His name. I fall so far short. I feel like I'm just beginning on the path of faith. Every day when I go to the set I realize how mortal I really am." He paused, "How can mortal man portray immortality?

"I count it a privilege to be one of His followers," he said. He leaned back in his chair. "I would say that I'm a Christian. Maybe not in the same sense that others talk about, but God means a great deal to me; even more since Tom and I speak to Him so often."

Tom Panella was an American Jew who had accepted Jesus as his Messiah and had come to Israel for one reason: to land a job so he could witness to his Jewish brothers and sisters. As Brian's stand-in Tom developed a steady friendship with the actor, praying with him before each scene and planting himself somewhere nearby to pray while they were filming.

Every day Tom stood in for Brian while lighting was adjusted and camera angles decided on. The scene usually involved the disciples and since the adjustments being made could take an hour or more, Tom used the time explaining the scene and talking with these men about the spiritual significance of what they were shooting. The disciples often asked questions of him and he was only too glad to tell them what he knew. It was obvious Tom Panella was doing his part in "tending to the harvest."

* * *

By the time we had been in production nearly six months it seemed any direction we turned unearthed a problem. The cast and crew were exhausted from working so long and hard. Except for a one-week break at Christmas, the crew of twenty-eight from England had been away from their homes nearly a half-year straight. Several actors had other contracts, and it was becoming increasingly difficult to keep everyone happy.

I prayed a great deal for John Heyman those last few weeks of filming. The demands on him had always bordered on superhuman. Now they seemed to double. He was everywhere at once: pacing, checking, answering questions, adjusting, encouraging. The film was a labor of love: "to God from John." And there was nothing he would not do to make things easier on someone else.

Filming the crucifixion scene was arduous, and painstaking in detail. Brian was strapped to the cross for over four hours. John carefully watched the progress of the scenes, on guard for Brian, gauging how much more the actor could give to the scene without giving too much. At one point there are several scenes shot from behind the cross, looking over Jesus' shoulder into the faces of the disciples, Mary and the soldiers. The man on the cross in those scenes is John Heyman.

To accelerate completion John hired a second camera unit. During the last months of filming, the two crews pushed daily from before daylight to nightfall. John personally directed the second unit all day, then held production meetings at night and somehow still found time to view the daily "rushes." Each night the new film, shot that day, was shipped out on an overnight flight to London. Each morning the developed print from two days before was delivered. Watching the edited "dailies" was a nightly ritual for John. Did we get the shots we wanted? Do we need to shoot again?

Gradually it all began to take its toll, and during the final month of filming John was in continuous physical pain. He suffered from an inflamed kidney, an acute stomach disorder, colitis and other things that he told no one about. Yet he pushed on, negotiating, cajoling, leading, directing at the very limit of human strength.

John was waking each morning coughing up blood. He had worked himself beyond the point of exhaustion, paying a dear price to see this film become a reality. He had given everything he had — financially, emotionally and physically. What would happen if John should collapse? Who would finish the film? It was *John's* dream. There was no one else. I doubled my daily prayers for him. We had come so far, but would we ever finish? Some days it seemed impossible.

CHAPTER SEVEN
2,000
OPENING NIGHTS

"This film is two hours of peace in a world of chaos," Larry said. One of Warner Brothers' top executives, Larry is a quiet man, capable, decisive and powerful in his position, but as he left the studio's premiere screening of *JESUS* that day he said, "I'd like to talk to you sometime, Paul, about Jesus. . .the man Jesus, not the film."

Several days later I dropped in to see him in his office. He pushed his chair back from the desk and looked at me. "How would I begin?" he asked, "I mean, with faith in Jesus?"

"Can you close the door and hold your calls for a few minutes?"

Larry shut the door and pulled a chair up beside his desk for me. "Maybe you need to know something about me first." He leaned back and looked off into the distance as if remembering.

"Several years ago in New York, my little girl was born with a hematoma on her head. The doctors explained it as a kind of huge blood blister. They said she would

be fine, but just to be sure, my wife and I hired a nurse
to sit with her during the night through the first few
weeks. The registry sent us one of those 'born-again'
people, the first one I had come across.

"You have to understand, Paul, I don't know much
about Christianity or Christians. Both my wife and I are
Jewish, although we hardly ever go to temple. We've tried
a few times since we came to California but they usually
have Milton Berle or some other celebrity reading the
Torah and it just loses its meaning for me.

"Anyway, one night when this nurse was still in our
home, I walked by my baby's room and looked in. There
was this Gentile woman beside my daughter's bassinet,
praying for my baby. I couldn't understand why a Christian
lady would pray for my Jewish baby."

Larry stroked his salt and pepper beard, still trying
to understand the love he had seen that night. I could
sense a longing in him to love the way that Christian
nurse had loved his child.

He looked back at me. "My daughter survived, and
we moved out here to Hollywood, but a short time after
the move my wife developed breast cancer and was seri-
ously ill. She underwent a radical mastectomy and the
doctors told me they were afraid she would not survive
the surgery."

Tears slipped into his eyes. "I wanted to die," he said.
"I wandered the city trying to find someone I could turn
to, someone who could help me face what was happening.
Finally I went to the synagogue hoping I could talk to
the rabbi; it would have helped so much just to talk to
someone. But it was Bingo Night and he was busy calling
numbers, so I walked out and wandered on down the street.

"The next thing I knew, I was standing in front of a church. It was dark, and locked up, but the lights were on in the parish house next door. So I knocked on the door and asked the priest if I could pray in the church. He got his keys and we talked a few minutes while he opened the church for me. He said he would pray for my wife.

"Early the next morning I was headed down the halls of Cedars of Lebanon Hospital toward my wife's room when a nurse stopped me. She said she was surprised to find out I had a mixed marriage. I couldn't understand why she'd think that, until she told me a priest had been at my wife's bedside since late the night before.

"I couldn't believe it. A Christian minister had come to the hospital and had sat with a sick Jewish lady he didn't even know. *Why? Why would he do that?*"

I listened as Larry opened the questions he had carried for so long inside him. "Thank God, she lived," he said, "but about four years ago she had a stroke and now requires continuous care. I hired a full-time housekeeper, a black woman from Watts. Turns out she was a born-again Christian, too, and for the last four years she's been telling me nearly every day that I need to get Jesus into my life." He smiled. He obviously liked his housekeeper. "On the weekends her sister came to relieve her, and she said the same thing. Every morning she'd say a prayer at breakfast . . ." His voice trailed off, and I realized he was choking back tears.

"Two weeks ago my housekeeper died," he said. He looked at me, "Now I don't know where to turn. I think what I need . . . is to get Jesus in my life."

I shared the gospel with him very quickly. He did not need a sermon. He had had the truth lived before him

for years. As we finished talking about the Four Spiritual
Laws I asked, "Would you like to pray this prayer of
invitation?"

"I really would," he said.

With emotion thick in his voice, Larry prayed a very
simple prayer of invitation to the Lord.

                              * * *

But before Larry or anyone else could experience the
message of *JESUS*, months of hard work and long, grueling
hours went into the completion of the film. There were
times when we thought production would never end, but
one day the director shouted, "That's a wrap!" and for
the last time cameras and crews shut down and started
toward home.

After seven months of pressure and fatigue, working
in Middle Eastern temperatures from freezing to frying,
our weary little "family" disbanded forever. The last frames
of *JESUS* had been captured. The impossible had been
achieved!

The filming phase was complete, but now came the
real work. Back in the studio every voice had to be
re-recorded to eliminate the background noise of a modern
civilization — the sounds of aircraft overhead, street traffic
and the blasting of horns. When the dubbing was done,
the task of editing the rough cut of the entire film began.

The pre-sale of discount tickets to churches and Christian organizations was well under way. Our goal was to
sell two million tickets in advance of the box office
opening to insure that local operators would keep the
film showing for several weeks.

Inspirational Film Distributors was formed to handle
all the pre-sale details, and began turning out brochures,

posters, flyers, and advertising in preparation for the six hundred committees to be established in cities across the United States.

We doubled our prayer efforts. The musical score was completed, recorded and wonderful. It was beginning to look as if things were finally coming together, and with our deadline bearing down on us it was none too soon. As long as nothing else happened.

* * *

The phone call came early on a Monday morning. A Christian attorney said *JESUS* was a film of heresy and threatened to obtain an injunction against us. He had heard that we had filmed the crucifixion scene without a crown of thorns on Jesus' head, and he was accusing us of trying to change the Scripture. Luke does not mention the crown of thorns in his account, but the lawyer would not accept that as reason enough. He would see us in court.

* * *

In September the first completed print of *JESUS* arrived in New York. In Warner Brothers' screening room sat key management people, a few lawyers and our Christian attorney friend who was threatening the lawsuit.

The story was clear, believable, accurate and spellbinding. It was, indeed, the undecorated Word of God brought to life, and its power struck awe in my heart.

Before the lights went up the attorney leaned over and said he was happily dropping the suit against us. . .

For the next several weeks I met daily at Warner Brothers with executives from advertising promotion, publicity, marketing, sales, accounting and financial control to map out the best plan of attack, name the film's strong points, and design our campaign.

Several times different ones approached me to talk about the man Jesus, not just the film. It was an exciting privilege just to share what Jesus had done for me, and I sensed an openness to what I had to say. They wanted to listen because they knew I was not trying to sell them something, or use them to work my way into the business. Almost daily I saw evidence that *JESUS* was producing a harvest and it had not even been released yet!

Executives and producers at the top live life in the fast lane — the rounds at all the parties, premieres and travel, all the perks — but no room for failure! With $15-25 million dollars at stake on every picture made, there is constant pressure on them to perform, and so they live with relentless tension, and the push for the *right* advertising and merchandising, the *right* release dates, the *best* theaters and the *biggest* guarantees on down the line. They cannot survive in their competitive world without them.

One of the key executives I met during visits to Hollywood was Tom. He was a success in many ways yet somehow seemed lonely. When we spoke he admitted to an emptiness in his life that gnawed at him.

On an ordinary afternoon over lunch in the commissary, Tom bowed his head and invited Christ to fill the emptiness in his life. Actors in bizarre costumes, producers, and crew members surrounded us, but our little table had become like a quiet chapel.

When he had finished praying I asked Tom, "Where is Christ now?"

He looked at me a moment, then smiled. "In my life, I think. At least I've asked Him to come in."

I turned to the back of the Four Spiritual Laws booklet we had been reading together and read 1 John 5:11 and 12.

"And the witness is this," he read, "that God has given us eternal life, and this life is in His Son. He who has the Son, has the life, he who does not have the Son of God does not have the life."

"Who is the 'Son' the Bible is speaking about here?" I asked him.

"Jesus."

"What kind of life do you have if you have the Son, Tom?"

"Eternal?" He sounded unsure.

"That's right," I said. "So what kind of life do you have right now?"

He smiled again. "Eternal life!"

"When does it end?"

"Never!"

"And when did it begin for you?"

"Just a few minutes ago," he said, "when I asked Christ into my life." He looked off into the distance, thinking things through, and I waited.

"Tom," I asked finally, "which of the people in this dining room would have eternal life?"

He looked at the faces around us, some hidden behind heavy theatrical makeup, others just as hidden behind pretense and fear. "Those who have Christ would," he answered slowly, ". . . only those with Christ." Tom was beginning to understand.

* * *

It was October, 1979. Premiere showings were under way in 250 cities across the United States. Pastors and church leaders were invited for advance screenings, and committees were then established in thousands of churches to sell the discount tickets. But Warner Brothers was worried.

One week before opening they realized that more than five million ticket coupons were in circulation. What if the coupons were used at the theaters and no money came back from the committees? Warner Brothers could lose millions! For several days I answered questions from key executives at the Burbank offices and eventually from some of the vice-presidents in the New York headquarters.

No problem, I assured them. These were Christian people they were working with — they would not keep the money.

Shortly after that we received news that a chairman from Idaho had pocketed $15,000 in ticket money and disappeared. After several long hours of deliberation, Warner Brothers finally agreed to accept the promise of other committee members in the Idaho area to make good the missing funds.

We opened October 19th in 250 theaters. By Tuesday the 23rd the weekend results were in. Warner Brothers was thrilled! Crowds were being turned away in twenty cities!

It was not just the evening crowds that were large; the matinees were also doing well, thanks to the United States Catholic Committee. Anna Greves, an educational consultant from Akron, Ohio, had organized a massive effort to bring Catholic school children to special morning and afternoon matinees. An office staff of ten in Akron worked around the clock to get tickets to thousands of schools and to make sure the managers were there to open the theaters for the special morning shows. By the end of the theater run more than 250,000 Catholic school children had seen *JESUS*.

In addition, the communications office for the U. S. Catholic Charismatic Renewal shipped tickets to prayer group leaders all over the country. Sister Rosemary in San Bernardino, California, sold more than eight thousand tickets herself.

Stories began to filter back from all over the country of those whose lives had been changed because of seeing the film:

The whole class got to go to the theater to see *JESUS*. On the bus the teacher said she would talk to anyone who wanted to know Jesus personally if they would see her after school. In the next two days she led fourteen of her students to Christ.

He was dying of cancer. As a final offering to the Lord he loved, a Campus Crusade staff member in New Jersey set up committees for theaters all over the city. He hid away in the projectionist's booth in one crowded theater and watched the film from there. Halfway through the showing he led the projectionist to a saving faith in the Jesus of the film.

In Birmingham and Jacksonville, Alabama, theater managers gave their lives to the Jesus they met in the picture. "I knew the people connected with the film could explain to me the real meaning of life," one said. "I was ready for them when they came."

A special screening was arranged on a college campus in Sacramento, California, where twenty-one young people indicated a desire to follow Christ and another fifty-two signed up for local Bible studies after seeing the picture.

A rating board member of the Motion Picture Association of America made a special phone call to our offices. "I must tell you," he said, "I have seen almost every film made on the life of Christ and this is without a doubt the finest of them all."

By Christmas more than two million people had seen the film. One year later when the run in commercial theaters finished, over four million people had witnessed the life of the man Jesus. We sent follow-up letters and gospels of Luke, provided by the American Bible Society, to thirty-five thousand people who requested more information on becoming Christians.

But numbers can tell only part of the story. If you could talk with a janitor from Atlanta, Georgia, he would remind you that the real story always unfolds in individual lives, like his.

A representative from Inspirational Films walked into the half-dark theater in Atlanta, and found the custodian kneeling down at the front, his broom leaning against the stage. "My wife's been telling me for years that I needed Jesus in my life," the janitor said, "I figured today would be as good a day as any, and I thought maybe one of you would tell me what to do."

CHAPTER EIGHT
THE MOVE OVERSEAS

JESUS had raised some gnawing questions in Roseann's heart when she saw it on TV in Swaziland. Her friend Jane MacKender would know the answers — she was on staff with Campus Crusade. Roseann invited Jane to her home with six other women, including two exotic dancers from a local nightclub. The women talked about Jesus for several hours and before the evening had finished all seven had prayed to receive Christ.

In Holland a lonely prostitute switched on the TV and discovered that a movie subtitled in Dutch had just begun. She got interested in *JESUS* and that night placed her faith in Him. She has left her old ways and is involved in a discipling ministry not far from Amsterdam's famous red-light district.

In South Africa the film was shown to mixed audiences of blacks and whites, and during its first two months more than 300,000 people saw *JESUS*.

A theater owner in Zurich, Switzerland, reluctantly agreed to schedule the film. "But only for a few days," he said. "I have to make a profit." Six weeks later nearly forty-eight hundred people had paid to see the film. Another city booked the film for eighteen days; fifty-nine hundred people attended with more than two hundred expressing an interest in becoming believers.

"*JESUS* outdraws *E.T.*" the headline read in an English paper. The classic Cinema in Westcliff reported ten thousand attended in four weeks time.

* * *

Long before these and the hundreds of other stories came to our offices, Inspirational Films began receiving requests daily from all around the world for copies of *JESUS*. With the wonderful results we had seen in the United States we were convinced that God intended to use it widely. Unfortunately that was about all we knew for certain. At least at the beginning, our questions about translating the film far outweighed our answers.

Several months after we began our foreign operations we received a copy of the following letter from Carroll Thompson, a member of one of the translating teams in India. He had written it to his supporters:

Hallelujah! Today we shipped the last of our Indian recordings off to London (ten of them from India plus one from Sri Lanka). Completing these translations has added a new significance to my life. Seven months ago I knew nothing about the film industry; today I feel like a seasoned professional, having accomplished the first major work I was sent to do. God has been good to us, and I feel tremendous satisfaction.

These last two months we worked sometimes day and night until the wee hours of the morning to meet our deadlines. Crises were common. We were trying to turn out one language after another as quickly as we could schedule the voice artist's time. Sometimes we had work in four languages going simultaneously.

The pressure is unending. I go home, but I dream about giving cues and eliminating mixer hiss. Every day holds a sense of suspense as we wonder whether we can complete the recording for this language before the artist's contracted time is up and he has to catch his train for home. But when that last line is said, everyone holds their breath to hear the right person yell "Cut!" Then the whole studio breaks out cheering! *Another language is complete.* We take pictures, go home and sleep well that night . . . and begin again the next day with a new group of artists, a brand new language.

The prints of the film are being made in London and shipped back. I may stay longer here in India to help with the rest of the project. Please pray for God's wisdom in making that decision. And pray for the touchiest part of this whole project, bringing prints of the film through customs and obtaining a favorable censor board rating. God is indeed doing a mighty work.

Getting new copies of the film into a country is a never-ending struggle with customs officials, many of whom promise cooperation if given large enough bribes. We determined early on that we would not pay bribes; instead we pray for free entry, paying duty only on the films as it becomes necessary. In Muslim or socialist countries, however, things are not always so straightforward.

Bangladesh is the second largest Muslim country in the world, after Indonesia. Just before our films arrived in Dacca, the capital, the government censor board banned the film *Ben Hur* calling it "too religious." Three days later, twenty copies of *JESUS* arrived at customs. A censor board meeting was scheduled, and the films were locked in a shed.

A few minutes before the meeting was to convene, Stephen, our coordinator, asked permission to go into the shed with the films.

"Why?" asked the guard.

"I want to pray over them," Stephen said.

Devout Muslims understand the importance of prayer, and so it was decided that Stephen should be permitted to pray over the films as long as he was watched the whole time. Flanked by guards, Stephen stepped into the dark storage shed and placed both hands on the metal canisters stacked on a table.

"Work miracles in this land, dear God," he prayed. "Work a miracle in the hearts of those on the censor board; let them pass this film even if they are not sure why they are doing it." No ceremony, no fuss.

Four hours later we were simply given our films and told that the Muslim censor board had passed the film.

In early showings in Bangladesh, Muslim opposition was expected to be heavy. But through the film, God touched the heart of a Chittagong army brigadier — himself a Muslim — to provide the film team with free military transportation, a military patrol, and an official letter of authorization to travel freely to the villages under his jurisdiction. The showings were a smashing success!

The brigadier told the team he had never seen such large gatherings in rural areas, or such zealous interest in a film. Chiefs of villages that had to wait for a showing often became angry and offended after learning other villages had seen it first. The response was overwhelming, far beyond our fondest hopes. Just one year after our first showing in Bangladesh, more than 586,000 people had seen the picture and nearly 250,000 had made decisions to know Christ. One itinerant pastor of thirteen small churches now shepherds over eight thousand people.

Why? One elderly pastor said that he had heard the gospel all his life but *JESUS* affected him and his people in a way nothing ever had. Perhaps it was because the words were in their mother tongue, speaking to them of someone named Jesus who understands their heartaches and touches their suffering.

It is difficult for those of us in the English-speaking world to understand what it means to someone in a small language population to see a film like *JESUS* in his own tongue.

The Princess of Tonga flew to London to give the film her final approval. As she watched the film and listened to the words of Jesus spoken in her own language, she wept openly.

On the Island of Vanuatu, all the key officials of the country were invited to attend the showing of the Bislama version previewed at the governor's palace.

The first showing of the film in the Republic of Burundi was held in the city of Bujumbura. As the local officials watched, they began to weep. One old man explained, "It is good to have the film, but look over there." He pointed to the young men operating the projector. "In the years and years of mission work done among our people, no missionary has ever permitted a national to touch the projector. Those are our own boys running the equipment!"

* * *

In the spring of 1980, the first translations of *JESUS* were begun. Cross-cultural introductions were prepared in certain languages presenting reasons a Hindu or Muslim could consider the claim of Jesus of Nazareth. Laboratories in Mexico City and Sao Paulo worked on Spanish and

Portuguese; French was prepared in Paris; Arabic recorded in London. But in Asia, under the leadership of Bailey Marks, director of Campus Crusade for Christ in Asia at that time, technicians launched a blitz that produced twenty-one language translations in eighteen months.

The goal for each translation was for the actors on screen, though originally filmed speaking English, to appear to be speaking the language on the sound track. This process of replacing a sound track with new sound, in this case another language, is called "dubbing." At every dubbing location, biblical, linguistic, theological and theatrical experts were assembled.

The first task was to answer several unusual but necessary questions: Can we edit Scripture? Which words should be omitted when the new language takes longer to speak than English? Which version of the Bible should we use? Who are the primary practicing Christians in the target country and which versions would they approve? How should the name *JESUS* be spelled? Which voice accent should *JESUS* have? Upper class? Lower class? Middle class? and on, and on. . .

Despite the challenges on every hand, translations proceeded at a tremendous pace. By 1985 more than one hundred language versions were completed. For the hundreds of small dialects we began to produce a narrative story-telling version using a single voice narration. These translations are much less expensive than the complete dubbing process.

We had initiated a plan to produce the film in every major language in the world, and we were making great headway, but new problems began to occur. As we progressed to the lesser known language groups, actors and qualified speakers became nearly impossible to locate in Los Angeles or London. Good directors whose mother tongue is Kanuri are scarce in California, and several translations had to be scrapped because we discovered too late that key speakers no longer spoke with pure accents since becoming Americanized.

As usual, God was already at work on the problem. Pierce and Lee Barnes came to work with us. Pierce was a long-time mission pioneer and back room technician and inventor as well. Almost immediately he started to work on an idea to simplify the dubbing process. Within a few weeks he presented us with a dubbing system that would enable us to set up a portable recording studio anywhere in the world, including the jungle.

The system is called computerized dialogue replacement (CDR) and connects a computer to a three-track videotape recorder. One track is the English dialogue from the film; the second is the computer time code; the third is an open track, ready to record the new language. Every line in the film has a seven-digit computer code which allows instant access to any line in the script.

For instance, if we want to dub in a new language to Peter's line, "Thou art the Christ, the Son of the Living God," we simply type in the code for that line. The computer finds it and begins moving the videotape back and forth over that line while the voice actor records the new language for this line over and over until the lip-synchronization is perfect. The first completed translation to be recorded this way was Estonian.

As the film was taken to different locations, each country presented its own special set of other problems to solve. For instance, out of respect, certain African tribes were uneasy watching the film until the old men pictured in various scenes were introduced. They assumed them to be important chiefs, elders in the tribes as they would be in their own, and were satisfied only when we explained that even the elders of the tribes in the time of Jesus were interested in His teachings.

To field test *JESUS* in Africa, we showed the film to nine different groups of students in the Republic of Malawi. They assumed the people they saw on the screen were the actual people written about in Scripture, and were surprised that a movie had been made two thousand years ago. Most had never seen a film and were shocked by close-up shots — they thought they were seeing a speaking head with no body. Medium shots looked like half people to them and also had to be explained.

Many had never seen a fish or a camel, and we learned that these had to be explained before the film began, or the message could be lost to curiosity over the strange creatures on the screen.

"Why do you call Jesus the Son of God if God never had a wife?" "Why don't Christians pray with their skulls down like Jesus does in the picture?" "Why did Jesus send the evil spirits from the demon possessed boy into the pigs and ruin the pig farmers' business?" "Does Jesus live in Nairobi?" "Who did they kill when they were making the movie?" Endless questions, but each one gave us the opportunity to be prepared with answers we would need when we took the film to untouched places.

And so the ministry of *JESUS* began to grow around the world.

And as the translations were prepared businessmen and their wives began to see that entire cultures and language groups could be reached quickly as the funds were available. Jerre Freeman, a doctor from Tennessee, and his wife Anne underwrote the twenty thousand dollar per language dubbing costs for Spanish, French and Portuguese. Wally Bruce, a retired contractor from Florida, financed the Farsi translation for Iran, Pidgin English for New Guinea and Quiché and Kekchi for Guatamala, and he helped with many others.

Jack and Barbara McClellan from New Mexico gave unselfishly to provide equipment for film prints for Africa and Latin America. And thousands of individual Christians, Sunday school classes and Bible study groups began sending monthly contributions to help support the teams who were showing the film.

JESUS ran on national television in Holland, Germany, Cyprus, Lebanon, Swaziland, Samoa, Sri Lanka, Peru, El Salvador and parts of India. In Madras it generated more response letters than any program they had ever shown.

Singapore ran *JESUS* in one of its largest theaters for seven weeks. More than two hundred thousand people saw the film, and nearly a thousand received Christ as Savior in the theater.

A mother in India wrote to her son who was away at school to tell him about the film she had seen about the man Jesus. With great joy she wrote, "Son, Jesus speaks Bengali!"

CHAPTER NINE
UGANDA

The sound of gunfire was getting closer. It was March, 1984. Since Idi Amin's overthrow, things were incredibly tense everywhere in Uganda. Rebel bands of marauders roamed widely now, flaunting their defiance, wearing it like a banner to be proud of.

The two young, white nurses from the clinic who showed the film *JESUS* in Kiryokya had just heard that men with guns had invaded the village a half-kilometer away. The sun was going down, and as Diana Langerock and Anita Wright turned the corner, a runner from the clinic nearly knocked them over in his haste to find them. They were needed right away.

The patient lay crumpled on the examining table in a pool of his own blood. He was just a boy, no more than ten years old, and he had been shot in the face. Three worried family members huddled together in a corner of the room watching the girls' every move. It was a bad wound, far too delicate for them to treat. He needed the immediate care of a surgeon but the nearest hospital was more than an hour's drive away.

"He's bleeding so heavily," Diana said. The urgency that she felt colored her voice.

Anita looked at her friend. "We've got to do something right now."

"Should we take him to Mityana?"

"We have no choice, Diana," Anita said. "But you know the nationals here at the clinic are going to think we're running from the soldiers."

"We'll just have to take that chance, I guess," Diana said. They would need medicine for him before they got to Mityana. She grabbed several vials and handed them to Anita. "Let's go."

Scooping the boy up in her arms she glanced at the three people who had come in with him. Without a word they followed her and Anita around behind the clinic and watched as she laid him gently in the back of her Suzuki pickup. Anita padded the boy with some extra blankets and the three relatives climbed into the bed of the truck, bracing themselves for the ride.

"Better take the back route," Anita suggested as she climbed into the cab.

"Good idea!" Diana headed out the back way. There had been no trouble on that road, so far, other than reports of bandits, and the soldiers at the roadblock were familiar with the girls' truck. As the only whites in the area, they were not hard to remember.

"What do we do if we're stopped by bandits?" Diana asked. She hoped she sounded matter-of-fact.

"I don't know," Anita said. "I guess we make a run for it."

Diana eased the truck into a wide turn in the road,

and in the half light of early evening thought she saw something moving in the road up ahead. She switched her headlights on just in time to cast them on a man with a gun coming up out of a ditch to the left of the road. Fearing an ambush, she stepped on the accelerator and prepared to move through the area as quickly as possible. She did not see the spindly branch stretched across the road until it was too late. They were through the barricade before they knew what they had hit.

Immediately gunfire erupted from both sides, and Diana stepped down as hard as she could on the accelerator. All she could think about was getting away. She slid down in the seat as far as she could and still see to drive. Anita and the people in the back ducked for cover and held on. The dirt road was slick with mud and she struggled to keep the little truck out of the drainage ditches on either side.

Gunfire seemed to come from everywhere and suddenly Diana knew the truck had been hit. The wheel jerked violently in her hands. Over her fear and the crackling sounds of gunfire, she yelled, "Pray!" Suddenly the road made a sharp turn and started down a steep incline.

"Thank You, Jesus! Thank You, Jesus!" Anita cried out over and over. All she could think of was how grateful she was for each moment they stayed on the road. Life was a gift straight from the hand of God.

Within a few moments they drove out of the range of gunfire and Diana regained control of the truck. They sped on in the growing darkness, weighing their options. There were not very many.

Surely the soldiers would pursue them. They knew they were in trouble there. Where could they go? How far could they get if the truck had been hit? Diana decided to stop long enough to see how badly the truck was damaged and to check on their patient in the back.

She pulled off the road and got out to look around. Anita tried to open the other door but it was jammed from the impact of the bullets.

The boy was frightened and still losing blood in great quantities. He would not last much longer. No one had been hurt in the barrage.

As Diana pulled the truck back onto the road she and Anita discussed what to do. Returning to Kiryokya was too dangerous, but neither of them knew a soul in the next town. Then Anita remembered meeting a woman from the village at a prayer group just the week before. It was a long shot, but they decided it was their only chance. It was getting dark, and they decided to develop a new plan of action if they found out this one would not work.

Anita went to the door and explained to the woman what had happened. In spite of the danger it meant to her and her family if they were caught, the woman opened her home to the fugitives and their patient. They carefully hid the truck in a coffee field behind the house and laid the wounded boy in a safe place. Then everyone settled down to wait out the long night.

The little patient looked bad. Bouncing around in the back of the truck had not helped his condition. He was bleeding badly again, and his breathing was restricted and shallow. The woman and her family gathered around the girls, the patient and his three worried family members and prayed. They prayed specifically that God would stop the bleeding, that He would let the boy breathe easily, and that He would allow him to sleep soundly through the night so that they could get him to a doctor in the morning.

Almost immediately the bleeding stopped. Within minutes the child had drifted into a peaceful sleep and was breathing normally.

Anita and Diana settled back to try to rest. They talked about what to do and decided to walk back to the roadblock in the morning to explain what had happened. They would tell the soldiers that they had not seen the barricade and had driven through it by mistake. They would tell them about the boy who had been shot.

A car drove slowly by outside. They were in a deserted area, far from well-traveled roads. Was it the soldiers looking for them? A few minutes later they heard shots nearby and an explosion. No one slept well that night.

Early the next morning word came to them that the soldiers were on their way. Before long, the commander of the roadblock was filling the doorway of the tiny house with his broad frame, demanding an explanation from Diana.

She whispered a prayer, took a deep breath and told the man exactly what had happened. He listened intently, able to understand English well. He understood too that the girls had meant no one any harm. Satisfied, he promised he would explain for them to the authorities.

The boy with the bullet wound woke rested and stronger. He walked to the truck, leaning on Anita's arm. They helped him into the back and took him the rest of the way to the doctor. Within a few short hours the bullet had been removed and he was well on his way to recovery.

Exhausted by the experience but exhilarated by the freshness of God's hand of protection on them, the girls headed back to Kiryokya that afternoon. As they approached the roadblock Diana slowed to a stop. Soldiers with guns were running toward the truck . . . shouting apologies at them.

"You must *never* run a roadblock again," they warned. "Someone might get hurt."

Again the women promised to be more careful, apologized for their mistake, and headed homeward, renewed and grateful to be alive.

Where do Anita Wright or Diana Langerock find the strength and endurance to continue giving medical aid and showing the film under stressful and dangerous conditions like these?

"We've learned so much about God's protection living here," Diana says. "One of the men at the roadblock told us that more than a hundred soldiers were firing at us that night. It's only the hand of God that kept us from being hit." She smiles, content where she is. "I guess I've learned firsthand that there's no safer place on earth than the center of God's will."

* * *

It was easy to see why Britain had once called Uganda the pearl of East Africa. Banana forests lay everywhere, remains of once flourishing plantations. The remnants of coffee and sugar plantations stretched as far as the eye could see in every direction, silent skeletons of a rich and vigorous history.

Idi Amin was gone but behind him he had left a broken and struggling country. The fingerprints of death were everywhere. The once life-giving Nile now flowed with the stench and filth of dead bodies against its banks; what had been a prolific animal population now struggled to survive. The few remaining banana plantations in operation faced the daily threat of bankruptcy and extinction.

Armed soldiers were a common sight in Uganda and no one escaped their presence. The nationals had lived in terror for so long that they seldom ventured from their homes after dark. Because of that, workers who had come to Kasaka ahead of us were just putting the finishing touches on the world's first "banana-leaf theater" when we arrived that morning. Hidden among the low hills was a little hut that would seat two hundred at a time for the showings of *JESUS*. The camouflaged theater, constructed entirely of broad, supple banana leaves tied to a bamboo frame, would make it possible to show the film all day long.

Before noon people began arriving, in twos and threes at first, then in slightly larger groups. Men left their work in the fields and came, carrying their machetes. Women and children came dressed in bright reds and yellows, brilliant oranges and blues, walking miles in their bare feet to get here.

It was a festive occasion, this showing of the film *JESUS*. The choirs from nearby Catholic and Anglican churches gathered to sing. Pastors from churches all around the area came, excited that *JESUS* had come to Kasaka at last.

One national pastor from several miles away said there had been an exciting increase in his congregation since the film had come to their area. Attendance had gone from less than thirty at services to more than six hundred within a year. The difference? Training that film teams made available to nationals, teaching them to share their faith. This pastor's congregation now had ten or twelve teams that went out daily to witness for Christ, and they were reaping a bountiful harvest.

"After we show the film," he said, "we write down

the names of each person who has accepted Christ, then our teams visit them in their homes. Often they begin Bible studies with them. We are finding so many more people interested in Jesus since we are showing the film."

"Do you need our help?" I asked.

"We could reach so many more if we had the film in other languages. We have the film only in Luganda," he said. He looked off into the cloudless sky as if seeing the future. "We could reach so many more if we had *JESUS* in other languages."

* * *

For thousands of Karamojong it is forever too late to hear the gospel. In 1980, 180,000 of these people died of starvation when raiders from the Sudan came down into Uganda and stole virtually every head of cattle; hundreds of thousands of them disappeared. Like their Masai neighbors to the east, the people of Karamoja had been herdsmen for centuries. The loss of their livestock threw the country into a state of famine within weeks. Driving through a northern section of Karamoja, I began to understand a small part of what had happened here.

Fields on either side of the rutted roads we bounced along were covered with the whitened bones of those who lay where they had fallen, victims of starvation. Walking sometimes for days in search of food, they had dropped by the way and died as others passed them by. More than a year later, their bones still had not been buried. There were too many.

We drove a few kilometers farther, and the driver stopped the car. Together we walked several yards off the road to a clearing where a chilling sight silently told its story. A pile of sun-bleached skulls lay clustered together. These men and women had not died of starvation; they had been executed for stealing food during the famine.

The pyramid of skulls lay in the scorching sun, a constant warning to others.

I picked up a skull in each hand, touching the reason for *JESUS*. How many of these Karamajong had had the chance to hear... before it was too late for them? More than seven years have passed, but the funds we need to translate *JESUS* into their language still have not been provided. Until someone cares — enough to give — the few faithful missionaries in Karamoja will have to continue the struggle to feed a spiritually hungry people alone.

CHAPTER TEN
BEIRUT BARRAGE

7:30 p.m.

I lay in the pitch black darkness of my hotel room pressing myself as tight as I could against the wall. The bricks were cold on my back and I ached from the hours of tension that kept my body rigid on the floor. Machine guns in the alley outside my room opened fire again and bullets flew past the windows, close enough that I could hear them slice through the warm air. Other guns returned the fire, and ricocheting shells snapped off the concrete buildings all around. With a terrifying, high-pitched scream, they sent deadly showers of flying particles in all directions. I held my breath, waiting for the windows to shatter. Instinctively I covered my head with my arms and buried my face in the musty hotel carpeting. There was nothing to do but wait it out.

After what seemed like a long time there was a brief let-up in the firing, and I seized the chance to inch my way across the floor toward my friend, Adel Masri. I kept my head down, crawling on my belly the way I had seen it done a thousand times in the movies. "Adel?" I whispered.

"Over here, Paul," he answered. I began moving in the darkness toward the sound of his voice. "Stay close to the wall," he warned. "There's less chance of getting hit if you keep below the windows."

"What's happening?" I could not hide the fear in my voice. I had come to Beirut to set up bookings for the film *JESUS*, not to get myself killed.

"I don't know," he answered. I was startled to hear how frightened Adel sounded. He lived here with the fighting and the danger. I had assumed you could "get used to it," but something told me now that no one ever did. My heart went out to Adel and his family as I began to realize what they lived with — every day of their lives.

"What're we going to do?" I asked. "Who's fighting who? Where are they?" Adel Masri was Lebanese; he lived in Beirut. Surely he would have the answers.

"I don't know," he said. "It changes every day. It's probably a new offensive by the Christian Phalangists. They want to get this area back from the Muslims, and this hotel is owned by Muslims." The firing seemed to increase, and Adel raised up on one elbow to peer out the windows overhead. In a second he had dropped back out of sight. "Looks like there's a machine gun nest right outside the window. We'd better just stay low till the firing stops."

"How long?"

"Sometimes only a few hours," he said. "Sometimes . . . much longer."

This wasn't even my war, yet I could get myself killed for staying in the wrong hotel. I began developing a plan. Machine gun bullets cannot go through concrete, I reasoned. If we took the mattresses off the beds and barricaded ourselves in the bathroom . . . surely the shells wouldn't be able to go through concrete and a mattress. I decided to present my plan to Adel.

As I opened my mouth to speak, a huge explosion violently rocked the whole building. Heavy artillery had rolled in and opened fire. Tanks were firing on the surrounding buildings and they were crumbling like pasteboard models. I decided not to mention my plan to Adel. All I could think of was the film clips I had seen on TV of the Beirut Holiday Inn a few months before. Hotels are not made for fighting wars in. They are places for vacations — just clean sheets and time to unwind and relax around the pool.

But wars never play favorites for Holiday Inns or little hotels like the one Adel and I were pinned in. One direct hit from the tank and the walls of this place would collapse all around us. My friend and I would be just two more poor unfortunates to die unknown in the night in war-torn Beirut, Lebanon. Had I come to this city to die?

In the midst of the gunfire, the phone on the nightstand across the room began to jangle. I jumped as if it were another explosion — phones are not supposed to ring during wars. I crawled toward it, keeping as low as I knew how.

I picked up the receiver, wondering who would call my room in the middle of a gun fight.

"It's me," the voice said, "George. I'm not going to make the meeting, Paul."

I glanced at the glowing numbers on my wristwatch and almost laughed. It was nearly eight o'clock. George was a Lebanese film distributor I was scheduled to meet with at 7:30 at my hotel. In the confusion I had forgotten all about it, but he was calling to explain why he was late.

"I started toward the hotel," he said, "and got caught

in a crossfire. I had to drive my car down the sidewalk to get away."

"Things have been pretty hot around here," I said.

"Now they've taken over my office building, so I can't even get at the contracts." He sounded more irritated than frightened. "Maybe I can collect them in the morning, Paul. I'll call you then. I'm really sorry this had to happen on your first trip to Beirut."

"What's happening?" I asked.

"Wish I knew. Might be the Phalangists, but I think more than likely it's some of the radical Muslim organizations fighting among themselves for control of this part of the city. One of the groups is headquartered in my office building and that seems to be near the center of the fighting."

"Well, we'll keep praying for your safety. Thanks for calling, George." I crawled back to my place against the wall, dragging the pillows off the beds with me this time. If we were going to have to stay here a while, we might as well be comfortable.

It was hard to believe I had only been in Beirut overnight. Adel had met me at the airport the morning before, dropped my things at the hotel, and taken me on a tour of the city. We drove slowly past the block-wide section of no man's land that stood between the Muslim and Christian sectors of the city. Syrian soldiers peered at us from sandbag bunkers lining the street.

"Why are the Syrians here?" I asked Adel.

"They're a peacekeeping force in the country until we can form some sort of coalition to run the government. The problem is that we have more wealth than Syria, and every week hundreds of cars are stolen and driven over the border into Syria."

"How do you know it's the soldiers?"

"Oh, they don't try to hide it. You can be driving along the road and ordered out of your car by a 'peacekeeper,' and that's the last you'll see of your car."

Adel slowed down to point out the American University to me. It had been established in the mid-nineteenth century by American Presbyterian missionaries as a means to exalt the name of Jesus and promote peace and understanding among the peoples of the Middle East.

"Yassar Arafat headquarters the Palestinian Liberation Organization in those student apartments over there." He pointed to some buildings near the road. "He lives here, and many of the P.L.O. fighters are students at the University."

"What's all the fighting about?" I asked. "Can anyone really explain it?"

"It isn't easy, but it's a Muslim-Christian thing, Paul. Lebanon has always had both factions, but when the Palestinians were driven out of Israel by the Jews, many of them came here. Arafat formed the P.L.O. in refugee camps to organize the Muslims. A few years ago they came into the city and simply took over the homes of some Christians in one of the sections.

"The P.L.O. wants to see Lebanon become a Muslim state but the Christian Phalangists are determined to see that it doesn't happen. Other Muslims, the Druse for instance, don't want Arafat in power; they don't even agree among themselves. In fact, there are twenty-seven different Muslim groups all vying for power. You never know who to trust in this city.

"It's really hard on my sons," he said. "Just walking

down the street they're challenged by the boys who fight for these groups to name which side they fight on. It's almost impossible to remain neutral here."

x x x

My second day there dawned clear and beautiful. Adel met me for breakfast at the hotel and we spent the next few hours in a marathon of meetings with key religious leaders, drawing together news releases and finalizing plans for the showings of *JESUS* in Lebanon.

Theater owners and distributors were excited about the film, not because they were fans of Jesus — most were Muslim — but because the film had been dubbed into Arabic. Most Hollywood films are translated only into the five or six major languages of the world. The time and money involved in translations for the smaller language groups are not profitable enough for the studios to underwrite the high costs. So countries like those in the Middle East usually receive films in English, or not at all.

By late afternoon we headed back to the hotel on foot. Not far from the American University Adel spotted a soldier he knew. "I wonder why he's here in Beirut. He's supposed to be down south on the Israeli border."

No sooner had the words left his lips than a sudden outburst of gunfire seemed to come from everywhere at once. I dove into the first open doorway I saw and landed sprawled across a couch, staring into the face of a man with a magazine. Feeling a bit sheepish I glanced around and discovered I was in an empty barber shop, sharing a couch with the barber.

"Don't worry so," he said, smiling down at me. "They're just trying to scare you."

"Well, I'm scared." I looked around for Adel. He was

coming through the door.

"You know why they do this?" the smiling barber asked me. I shook my head. "The fighting got worse outside the city today," he said, "and they need to bring the wounded into the hospital. We have no traffic police, so they fire a few rounds in the air, the cars drive up on the sidewalk, and the ambulances can get through." In an odd sort of way it made sense.

By the time we had walked the rest of the way to the hotel my heart was beating normally again . . . until Adel began to look around. "I don't like this," he said, more to himself than to me. "Something doesn't feel right."

"What is it?"

"I don't know really," he said. "Just a lot of little things. There are too many Phalangist soldiers in the city for one thing. Last week a large group of them defected to the Muslims. Rumor has it it's a 'Trojan Horse' operation. Some people think they're going to try to retake West Beirut from the inside."

Darkness was approaching quickly, and as we walked the last block together it suddenly felt as if we were the only ones on the street. "I think we'd better get inside," Adel said.

We went straight to the hotel dining room. Hardly anyone was there, just two or three couples and two other men at the bar. As Adel and I ate our dinner it became obvious that the men at the bar, an Englishman and an American, were edgy too and had every intention of drinking their fears away.

The first shots exploded right outside the window. "Let's get out of here," Adel shouted at me. I did not need to be convinced. "Stay away from the windows," he warned. I followed him up the stairs to my room on the second floor. We threw open the door and hit the carpet. We had not turned the light on; it would have made us perfect targets. And so now we waited in the dark, praying for the shooting to stop.

10:00 P.M.

The hours seemed endless. Did anyone even know we were here? How would we get away? Should we go to the U.S. Embassy? Where was it? Which direction would you run to get away from the shooting? Will we die tonight? If only they knew we were neutral . . . . *They need a "time out" so that all the people who are here in the war by mistake can go home.* But no one does that, and it hit me clearly, *these could be my last few hours alive.*

I began to take stock of my life, to ask the important questions like, how am I doing with God? We glibly say there are no atheists in foxholes, but I believe it must be true. This foxhole had a rug but my life was endangered. All that really mattered was my relationship with God.

Adel and I began to pray. As the firing increased around us, so did our prayers. We prayed alone, dealing with the private things we could not tell anyone but God; we prayed together for our own safety, for the soldiers just outside our building, for our families . . . Kathy, my wife, and the children. I wanted to talk to her just once more, to tell her that I loved her.

I crawled back over to the phone. "Adel," I whispered, "it's still working!"

"I must try to reach my flat," he said. "We don't have a phone but my neighbor can check on my family." Hours before, he had given up trying to make it home. Every street and alleyway between the hotel and his flat a few blocks away was filled with machine gun fire. He dialed a number and began talking rapidly in Arabic. I sank into my own thoughts.

Should I try to call Kathy back in the States? What would I say? Hi, honey, it's me. I'm caught in a war. Try not to worry. In case I die I want you to know I love you . . . No, I couldn't do that. Besides, God would probably save our lives and I would have scared her for nothing.

Adel hung up the phone, and I waited, fearing the worst. "So far they are all right," he said. "My neighbor crawled down the stairs and found out that no one is hurt. Oh, Paul, I'm so worried. The fighters have set up a rocket launcher on the roof of our flat and are attacking another group a few blocks away. The other side is firing back and shooting our building to pieces with my family inside . . . "

Adel knelt with his face to the floor and for the next few minutes cried out to God in Arabic, pouring out his fears, pleading for the safety of his loved ones.

12:30 A.M.

The firing seemed to let up for a time and Adel suggested we try to see what was happening downstairs. Hugging the walls, we crept down toward the lobby. From the stairs we could see a soldier patrolling the doorway of the hotel. He wore fatigues and carried a Russian-made Kalishnakov. Several loose belts hung across his broad shoulders, holding rounds of extra ammunition.

From a corner in the bar came the blended voices of the Englishman and the American, singing in a slurred harmony, still drinking away the reality of the night.

Adel spoke with the hotel manager. The soldier at the

entrance was a mercenary, hired to keep the warring factions out. "The manager hopes that if he can keep both sides out of the hotel, he can save it from attack."

The firing became heavy again so Adel and I decided we would be better off back in my room.

2:30 A.M.

"Paul and Silas sang when they were in jail," he said. "Let's sing." My heart was not in it, but anything was better than lying in the darkness listening to the sound of guns firing outside the window. For the next hour we sang every song of praise and worship we could think of, and as we praised the Lord together, our spirits were lifted. We prayed, and with our arms around each other, claimed God's protection for Adel's family.

4:00 A.M.

Over the sounds of shooting, a voice could be heard, faintly at first, muffled with the gunfire. An armored car mounted with speakers drove slowly between the two factions. As it came closer the voice was clear — someone speaking Arabic, weeping as he spoke. Adel translated for me. Through the speakers came the names of the women and children whose husbands and fathers had been killed in the fighting. The broken voice begged the fighters to stop. The firing continued, but not as heavily.

5:00 A.M.

The last small arms fire ceased and the city fell quiet in the gray shadowed dawn. Adel peered through the window at the machine gun emplacements across the street. They were empty. "I must try to make it home," he said, and was gone.

I slipped into a troubled sleep only to wake within the hour to the ringing of the phone. It was George, the film distributor. He had gotten the contracts and would meet me for breakfast at 7:30. I hung up and was thinking about a shower when Adel called. The windows had been shot out in his apartment, they had no electricity, and he was moving his family and food to another location — but everyone was all right.

10:00 A.M.

Contracts were signed and the opening dates set for three theaters in Lebanon at Christmastime . . . providing the theaters were still standing by that time. I offered the cab driver a little extra money to get me to the airport. He was reluctant but said he would try.

As Beirut rolled past my taxi window, my heart was heavy. So many buildings lay in rubble along the street; seventy-five cars had been blown up during the night; thirty-four people had been injured; twelve had died.

For some reason, God had stayed the hand of death in a small hotel room near the war zone of Beirut. For Adel Masri and Paul Eshleman there would be another day to serve Him.

CHAPTER ELEVEN
THAT'S INCREDIBLE

In the Solomon Islands a little girl played quietly on a thatched mat under a shade tree while the sun teased through the leaves, sprinkling itself on her shining, black hair. She wrapped her frail arms around her doll, hugging it against her, rocking slowly back and forth. Ever so softly she hummed the lullaby her father had sung to her forever.

"Time for a nap, baby," she said. Tenderly she tucked her doll under a cloth and curled up beside her. She was tired, too, so tired. It was even hard to breathe sometimes.

The child's mother leaned against the doorway of the house watching her daughter. Five short years. It wasn't enough. How was she ever going to give her up? She choked back the tears that seemed ready to spill down her cheeks every minute lately, ever since the doctors had told them that their little girl was dying. She and her husband lived every day with the fear that that would be the last time they would hold this child of their love, their little girl.

That night Mother and Father scooped the child into their arms and took her with them to see a film called *JESUS* that had come to their village. There was so little joy in their lives right now. A few hours of entertainment might make them all feel better.

The child sat in her father's lap during the showing, her head leaning against his chest as they watched Jesus heal sick people and raise Jairus' daughter from the dead. Their faith was new, but this was the same Jesus on film that they had invited into their lives. If He could heal the sick and raise the dead when He walked this earth... He could do it now!

She was already asleep when they laid her on her bed that night. For a moment they looked at her in the half-darkness, then joined hands and knelt together beside their child.

"Jesus," the man prayed, "tonight in the film we saw You raise that other little girl from the dead. We know You can heal our daughter, and we are asking You to do that right now."

The little girl slept peacefully through the night and woke ravenous the next morning. The luster had returned to her eyes, her spirits were high again, and she chattered like a wild bird in a banana tree. Fully confident that God had healed their child, they took her to the doctors for confirmation. The doctors could not explain the sudden turn in her condition.

Smiling, her parents gave them the answer science could not find: She had been given back to them by God. He had healed their child.

* * *

In a small village in India, a couple who had attended

a showing gave their neighbor a flyer about the film. It bore a picture of Jesus, and the man wondered whether *this* might be the one true God, *the God they should worship*. With his wife and children watching, he tacked the flyer to the wall of their hut, wishing they could know more of the smiling God in the photograph.

Months passed, and one afternoon a small group of college students gathered at the door of the hut. They were in evangelistic training with a local film team, and their assignment that day was to "practice" talking to people about Christ.

A girl on the team noticed the yellowed flyer hanging on the wall inside. "Oh!" she said with some excitement, "You're Christians!"

"No," the man said. "We are not."

"But the picture of Jesus on your wall," she said, "I thought . . . "

He glanced over his shoulder. "We have hoped someday to learn about this man. We have heard only that He is the one true God, but there is no one who can tell us about Him."

The group on the porch just smiled. "We can tell you," someone said. The man invited them in and together with his wife and children he heard the Good News of salvation. Before the team moved on, the entire family had prayed to receive Christ into their lives..

* * *

In the village of Djurukturu, Indonesia, the witch doctor crept quietly into the back of the room where *JESUS* was being shown. For a few minutes he watched the screen, listening to the scriptural dialogue being spoken in his language. He looked around the audience at the upturned faces of his people. They were listening. They were hearing God's word. He made a quick and quiet exit.

Just outside the door he spat on the ground. *They will pay! These foreigners who bring God in this way are not needed in our village; my people do not want this so-called gospel. I will make them pay!*

He rushed back to his hut and covered the windows from curious eyes. Inside he set to work, creating a curse that would finish these interfering foreigners and the fools who believed what they said. He would induce Satan to make them all so ill that they would die for their foolishness. His work completed, he sat back to wait until the fun began.

The showing ended and finally nearly everyone who had stayed to talk to a team member was heading home. But they all looked well. The witch doctor was puzzled. Perhaps it would take more time. Then several of the villagers stumbled into the clearing near his hut — not those who had been foolish enough to "believe" that night, but several who had not. They writhed on the ground and cried out from the intense pain in their bodies.

A film team member crouched down and laid his hands on one of the sick men. As he prayed for the man, the pain began to ease, and finally disappeared. It was happening that way all around the village now. Those who were suffering could be healed only if a film team member or a new village convert prayed for them.

The witch doctor's curse had been successful, with the exception of one small oversight. In cursing believers, he had brought the curse against himself and others who had not believed. He had not known how well God protects His own.

* * *

To those of us "older," more westernized believers, voodoo and demons, healings and angels are somewhat "out of the ordinary" and a little hard to believe. Certainly we acknowledge that God can still work miracles — after all, He is the same yesterday, today and forever. But it is still a bit baffling to some of us "conservative" folks to hear what is happening in other parts of the world.

Not so among the new believers! To those who know nothing more of Jesus than what they see in the film, it seems perfectly logical that the miracles they witness in *JESUS* might have occurred last week. If Jesus could do those things for the people of the village He visited in the picture, is there any reason to believe He cannot do the same for them?

During the '70s American films dealt a great deal with demons and the occult, but since that time we have seen a decline in the emphasis on these things, as if it were some kind of spiritual fad. Some would say that the great awakenings in many parts of the United States and Canada have created a movement of demonic activity to other parts of the world. Others would say that Satan is alive and well, but our level of spiritual sophistication keeps us from acknowledging such wild concepts.

In many areas of the world, however, demon activity is a daily occurrence, and two of the most relevant scenes in the picture are those where Jesus casts out the demons from the wild man of the Gadarenes, from Luke 8, and the story of the demon-possessed boy, found in Luke 9.

Reports of unexplained miracles started coming in from around the world, and I began to check into the facts, documenting everything possible. What has happened is truly *incredible*!

* * *

A Christian woman in the United States had been given just a few weeks to live. Cancer had been found throughout her body in such advanced stages that she was beyond the reach of surgery and chemotherapy. Both she and the doctors had given up hope, and she was preparing to die.

As she sat through a showing of *JESUS*, her focus shifted to the Christ being brought to life before her. He was the God of the living who healed the sick and the lame. He was the God she served, and He was able to heal her — that day. Sitting in the darkened theater, she simply believed God for her complete healing.

She was scheduled for more medical tests the next day, and her doctors were dumbfounded by the results. Not one test showed a trace of the cancer that had filled her body just the day before. More tests were run, but no cancer could be found. God had kept His promise to His child.

* * *

The Reverend S. Dinakaran is a Nazarene pastor in Whitefield, India. He and his team took the film to a small village on the outskirts of town. The equipment was set up and the film running when suddenly everything went dead. The projector had gone on the fritz. As the team members packed up their equipment, they promised to return the next night with a cooperative projector and show the film as planned.

The villagers wandered away from the scene, except for one young boy who approached the team as if he had something to say.

"It is no accident," he said. "It is the Sathya Sai Baba. He has cursed the showing of this film. My friend who is a follower of Sai Baba has said it is so." Sathya Sai Baba is a self-proclaimed savior and messiah with twenty million followers.

The second night the team returned well-prepared, with three working projectors. But as they set up the screen, trouble began again. Twice the poles used to hold the screen broke in half — these poles are made of iron. Resourcefully, they tacked the screen to the side of a building, but just as the last nail was hammered into the wall, an unexplained tear appeared at the top of the screen as if it had been slashed with a sharp knife. They had to stop again to make repairs.

Finally ready to begin, they turned the projector on and immediately the bulb burned out. Grateful that they had brought another, they threaded the film on the second projector, but the bulb on it blew out as well.

By this time the team was frightened, so they stood together and prayed that God would protect and deliver and would cast out the evil spirits so obviously at work against them. While they prayed, a man in the audience jumped to his feet and ran from the group. He was identified as a follower of Sathya Sai Baba.

The last projector was turned toward the screen and switched on, and *JESUS* continued without further incident. Later a group of Christians who had traveled from Bangalore to Whitefield Centre that night said that they had sensed strong demonic power at that time.

* * *

After finishing a showing of *JESUS* in a rural village in Thailand, film team members decided it would be wiser to sleep there than to try to make the trip home in the darkness. Although they had not been warmly received by the villagers, they felt sure they would be given a safe place to stay for the night.

They were told they could sleep in the Buddhist temple; they were not told that this temple was known for miles around for its inhabiting demons. Others who had tried to stay there either had been run out before morning or had been found dead the next day.

The team gathered their equipment and settled down on the floor of the temple. Shortly after drifting off to sleep they were awakened all at once by the immaterial presence of a hideous beast. There in the corner of the room appeared the most frightful image they had ever seen. Fear struck them all like an icy fist.

"Let's do what Jesus does in the film," someone shouted. So together they prayed, and cast the demon out of the temple *in the name of Jesus*! Sensing that the demon had lost his power in the presence of the Son of God, the entire team fell into peaceful sleep.

Early the next morning the villagers came to the temple to look for the team's equipment. They were certain that, like the others, these too had been driven away in the night, or killed. When they found them all sleeping undisturbed, they were confronted with the undeniable fact that God is more powerful than any other force.

* * *

Near a village in Thailand where *JESUS* was being shown, a gang of thugs decided to rob the team of their equipment, hock it and make some quick money. Creeping into the village during the night, they scouted the hut where the team's equipment was stored. Security was simple. It would be an easy job.

But as they approached the entrance, they were startled by two brilliant white beings filling the doorway. Both were over eight feet tall and brandished flaming swords. Frightened, the robbers ran into the darkness.

Hiding in the bushes, they convinced themselves that they had probably seen a ghost and decided to try again. They went around to the back door this time, but again the figures appeared, blocking the entrance, keeping them from what they had come to steal.

One of the robbers cried out, "If this is the power of their God, we dare not steal from them!" Later, some of the gang members ventured into a film showing and became believers. It was one of them who told this story to the team.

* * *

One team in Burma was crowded into a public bus traveling a mountainous road to show the film when the bus slipped off the edge of a cliff and tumbled over and over to the bottom of a gully. All the passengers required hospitalization . . . except the three men on the film team. Even their equipment had been kept from harm.

At another location in Burma, a staff member was presenting the invitation at the end of the film when a poisonous cobra slithered out of the underbrush and onto his feet. The audience held their breath as the man prayed that God would demonstrate His power and protect him from the viper. As quickly as it had come out of the jungle, the serpent slipped away again, leaving the man unharmed and onlookers in awe of the power of God.

* * *

Our director in Thailand took a team into the most dangerous part of southern Thailand where bandits roam the countryside, stopping travelers to rob and kill at will. These bandits are better armed than the military and are not known for their patience. It was for good reason that the staff was afraid on this trip, and fears mounted with every mile.

Finally the director pulled off the road to let the car behind them pass, and to pray for peace and safety on the rest of the trip. Back on the road they soon caught up with the car that had passed them a few minutes earlier. It sat on the side of the road engulfed in flames. All the occupants had been killed.

They continued driving, grateful for the Lord's protection, but deeply troubled by the deaths of the people in the car. A few miles farther, they came upon a truck that had been pillaged and destroyed in the same manner. A second time they had been spared.

Not sure of the route to the village, the director decided to take the left fork in the road. They discovered later that if they had taken the right side of the fork, it could have been their car that was blown up and the occupants killed instead of the car just behind them.

God spared their lives and used them to provide the gospel in film to several thousand searching people in southern Thailand for whom there might never be another chance.

* * *

" . . . You will seek the Lord your God, and you will find Him if you search for Him with all your heart and all your soul" (Deuteronomy 4:29).

Sitting in the audience of a *JESUS* film showing in Mandala, India, was a bhaghat (witch doctor) who recognized the fact that Jesus was a powerful God. In a flyer about the film he found a photograph of this Jesus, and, taking it home, he carefully placed it with the pictures he already had of other gods and sacred beings that he worshipped.

He stepped back and looked at the assortment of deities lined up on his shelves. He wondered, could they really all be gods? The god in the film he had seen that night had such wonderful powers, and He claimed to be the one true God.

Starting at the beginning he looked carefully at each face. Some were beautiful, some grotesque, but finally he was looking again into the eyes of the man Jesus. They could not all be the same, he reasoned. There had to be one God who was more powerful than all the rest, and He would be the one true God. Yet how would he know which one it was? A test. That was the answer, a test that only the most powerful God of all would be able to pass.

The searching bhaghat laid a tiny ball of dried cow dung, a common fuel burned in India, directly in front of each picture. He believed that only the one true God would have power enough to ignite the ball of fuel that sat before his picture. He put the last of it out and stepped back to wait.

Almost immediately the bit of fuel in front of the picture of Jesus burst into flame and burned until it was gone. It was the only one and it was enough to convince him that Jesus was the one true God he longed to know. Without a second thought, he rid his home of the false gods he had worshipped, and now he spends much of his time sharing with the other bhaghats of his city how it is he is so sure that Jesus is the one true God.

CHAPTER TWELVE
BUT DO THEY LAST?

The village of Pamongan is in the heart of the oldest Islam settlement in all of Indonesia. The first fiery Muslim missionaries had swept across this part of central Java nearly six hundred years ago, choosing Demak, a nearby city, as the site of the first mosque to be built in the country. No Christian church had ever existed in this steamy farming village, and frankly, none of the churches in the Semarang region had even considered doing evangelism here. Early attempts had all failed miserably. Pamongan was "closed" to the gospel and everyone knew it. So God began to work from the inside.

In Pamongan, Muslim merchant Subawi had grown restless in his quest for God. Frustrated in his search for lasting peace of mind and troubled by his crippling weakness for gambling, Subawi pestered the local mullahs (Muslim teachers) for answers every chance he could. Questions burned inside him like an unquenchable flame.

For weeks he sought help from the mullahs but the rituals he was told to perform and the laws they instructed him to live by never helped. Still he gambled; still he

117

had no peace. Where was the freedom he so desperately longed to know?

His questions increased until one afternoon the mullah threw his hands over his head in exasperation. "I do not have the answers you seek, Subawi!" he said. He pointed to the bookshelves lining his wall. "There. Take what you will from my shelves and find it yourself!"

Subawi looked at title after title, and the one called "Holy Bible" caught his attention. A friend had mentioned it to him a long time before. He lifted the black-bound book from the mullah's shelf, tucked it under his arm and headed for home.

Subawi had heard that a very powerful mullah named Jesus was written of in these pages; someone who had healed sickness and raised people from the dead. Surely this mullah would have the answers he sought so earnestly — if only he could find His name in the book. He opened it at the beginning, looking for the name of Jesus, but, turning page after page, he could not seem to find it. Then, almost at the end of the book in a part called the New Testament, Subawi found what he was looking for.

With a great hunger in his heart, he read the pages several times and knew this was the truth he had sought for so long. He was not sure how to make it a part of himself, how to draw it into his life, but he shared with his family what he had discovered in this wonderful book the Muslim teacher had loaned him.

Subawi's mother Sunarti, a widow now, was desperately afraid of dying. She lay awake at night worrying about the afterlife, the superstitions and black magic of the central Java culture casting fearful images into her mind. She had sought the answer to her fears through a shaman, a priest who uses magic. With his powers he could cure sickness, uncover secrets, see into the future, and control events in people's lives, but he could not reassure Sunarti about her fate after death.

When Subawi shared with his mother what he had read Sunarti knew he had found what they both had been looking for. Swandini, Subawi's brother, joined them as they named themselves Christians. Only Subawi's wife remained opposed to their ideas about this Jesus they spoke of. She treated them all as if they had gone mad.

Several weeks later, friends from Semarang told of a film they had seen in their village. It was about this man called Jesus. Subawi asked permission from the village chief to show the film in Pamongan too, but he was refused because there were no Christians to sponsor it. "I am a Christian," he said. "My mother and brother are Christians as well. We will sponsor the film together!" And arrangements were made.

A few nights later, the film *JESUS* was started for the first time in Pamongan. Within the first three minutes the amplifier blew out. After all the waiting and preparations, there seemed nothing else to do but cancel the showing, until a Muslim mullah in the audience offered the amplifier from the mosque. It was hooked up and the showing proceeded without a hitch.

At the end of the film, when the villagers were given the opportunity to receive Christ, Subawi, Sunarti and Swandini were the first to take a public stand for the Jesus they had loved for many months. Two others stood with them that night: a fifty-year-old laborer named Parti, and a Muslim mullah.

The next night some of the team members were to meet in Sunarti's home with those five who had taken a stand in their new faith, but eight people were there, including three who had been too afraid to stand publicly the night before. The little group met weekly and quickly grew to twenty, then fifty and soon to more than one hundred. One year later, Campus Crusade officially turned the Pamongan congregation of two hundred believers over to Baptist church leaders for supervision and pastoring. One active member of the congregation is the former leader of the mosque.

And Subawi's wife? She put up such an antagonistic resistance to his new faith in Christ that an evil spirit moved into their home. "My wife knew it well," Subawi told me. "We could not see it but whichever room it was in had the odor of a dead body, and you could tell when it moved from room to room. Every time I knew the spirit was there I would command it to leave in the name of Jesus and it would leave.

"Then one night a very influential family came to ask me to pray for their crippled son. I explained to them that I could not heal anyone, but that Jesus had the power to do whatever He chose to do. As I prayed, the family and my wife watched, and before our eyes the boy was healed.

"Another time my sister was in need of surgery to remove several painfully inflamed polyps from her face. I prayed for her too, and the Lord healed her as my wife looked on. It was all my wife needed. She opened her heart to Jesus too, and things have been good between us since then. Where she openly ridiculed me before, she respects me now in a way I have never known."

The church at Pamongan has faced pressures from Muslims, who tell them that those who call themselves Christians will be crucified on crosses when they die because that is the way Christians die.

"When we held our first baptismal service," Subawi

said, "they put poison in the pond. The surface was covered with dead fish, but we went ahead with our service and no one even became ill."

On another occasion, the chief tried to prevent villagers from attending church by ordering his bodyguards to beat them up. But for some unknown reason, the men beat him up instead and left him for dead. When the Christians of Pamongan heard what had happened, they went to the chief's house and prayed that God would heal him. He was restored to health and made a public statement of appreciation for what they had done for him.

* * *

With the hundreds of church buildings in the United States that sit empty on Sunday mornings, it is sometimes difficult for Americans to understand the excitement about church planting. But to those involved in foreign missions church planting is the reason they are there. So often, though, the methods used make it a futile effort.

The ambassador to the United Nations for Swaziland told me, "You missionaries do it all wrong when you come to our country. First of all, you start with the women. We are a patriarchal society. If you reach the men, the women and children will follow.

"Second, you bring too much written material. We have been working hard, but still we have only 28 percent literacy in Swaziland. Bring films, conduct dramas. Involve the children in plays about Jesus and the fathers will always come to see their children perform."

JESUS has proved to be an excellent solution to this challenge. Everyone comes when the film is shown in a village — it is a civic event, and often a novelty, since many of the areas where the film is shown do not even have electric lights.

After the showing everyone is given a chance to "come to the light" and receive Christ. *JESUS* serves as a filter to find those who are ready to accept Him as Savior. The film also presents the gospel clearly, greatly reducing the chance of leaving people with misunderstandings.

And teaching is begun the next day when follow-up sessions are offered to those who have professed Christ. New Christians are taught how to study their Bibles, how to share their faith, and how to continue meeting together for growth and edification. Out of these small groups have come new churches on every continent.

Paul McKaughan of the Presbyterian Church of America said, "The *JESUS* film is the greatest tool for evangelism that God has given the church in the last hundred years. I believe it is one of the finest church-plant ing tools we have ever had."

* * *

It was 6:30 in the morning and already the heat and humidity were noticeable — not quite unbearable yet, but it would come. After all, this was Indonesia.

We crawled into the van and started up the road to the little village of Stugur nestled against the foot of an old volcano about two hours drive out of Semarang. The road wound like a lazy snake through mile after mile of terraced farmland where for generations nationals had eased crops of rice, tapioca, coffee and bananas from the rich hillsides.

We turned off the main road and began to climb higher on one lane that was hardly more than a rock-covered back trail. Lush tropical growth closed in around us as we climbed higher, and the smell of damp soil was rich and cool. Rain fell lightly, then stopped, keeping the soil muddy most of the time and producing the wonders of the rain forest we rode through.

We were met by the chief of Stugur at the government town hall. It was barely 8:00 in the morning and already more than three hundred new believers waited for us inside the building. Some had walked long distances and nearly all of them had received Christ as a result of the *JESUS* film. We learned the story from the chief as he spoke through an interpreter.

Several months before, a film team had come to the area and asked permission to show the film in Stugur. The local chief was curious and agreed. When the showing had finished, both the chief and his wife prayed to receive the Lord.

In several areas surrounding the village, the film team had already established home Bible studies that were now pushing at their seams. So the chief opened Stugur's government meeting hall for follow-up sessions, further showings of *JESUS*, and combined meetings of all the groups on Sundays. Now they were a church of more than three hundred members, and they were excited about the fact that soon they were to come under the authority and direction of a denomination.

Pardji Priyons, a member of the church, was a Buddhist priest when *JESUS* came to Stugur. He had been a Buddhist since childhood and was a coordinator in his area of Kecamatan. His credentials among Buddhist circles were the finest: ordained as a Bishop at Candi Bord by Bibu Cjiro Gito in 1968, attended by National Buddhist leaders from outside the country; ordained as a Pandita Munda (young Buddhist priest) by 1972.

"As a priest, I tried very hard to live a holy life," Pardji said, "but worldly things always attracted me, so

I was full with sins. I gambled, drank and was involved with immorality. I had no peace within me at all. Instead, I was filled with emptiness and frustration, pretending to others that I was the holy man I was supposed to be. It affected my home too; I had no love for my wife and my family was in ruin.

"But, praise God, five months ago all that changed! Some visitors from the *JESUS* film team came to my house and explained the gospel to me. What touched my heart was that Jesus said in Luke 5:32 'I have not come to call righteous men but sinners to repentance' [New International Version]. I knew I was a sinner. And 1 Corinthians 13:13 touched a place in me too when I learned that the greatest thing in the world is love.

"Then the film *JESUS* came and the big change in my life took place. I am now sure about my salvation; even in my home Christ has proved His great love in my life to my wife and family. We have been married for twenty years, yet now I feel as if I have just taken a new bride.

"We have started a home church in my area now and eighty people attend. I will give the rest of my life to tell the children about Jesus."

The results of the *JESUS* ministry are remarkable. It is not just another collecting of "spiritual scalps." Follow-up counselors are found and trained long before the film is shown, and the home Bible studies and study groups that are organized afterward help those who meet Jesus through the film to grow in their new faith.

We are not seeing emotional responses to a moving film but decisions that change lives and breed the desire to share what they have found with those who do not know Him. It is pure, unbridled joy to be a part of this.

John the Baptist baptizing in the Jordan. An emotion-packed scene from the movie, *JESUS*, distributed to theaters throughout the world.

2. Jesus talks with Peter, James and Mary. Every scene in the *JESUS* film was shot on location in the Holy Land.

3. Feeding the 5,000. This film has now been translated into more than 100 languages throughout the world.

. Jesus throwing the moneychangers out of the temple. Jesus speaks no other words in the film besides those found in the Scripture.

"I will never leave you or forsake you."

6. Producer John Heyman prepares for closeup of Brian Deacon, the Shakespearean actor who portrayed Jesus.

7. Filming Jesus teaching from a boat on the Sea of Galilee.

8. Paul Eshleman's scene in the film lasted three seconds.

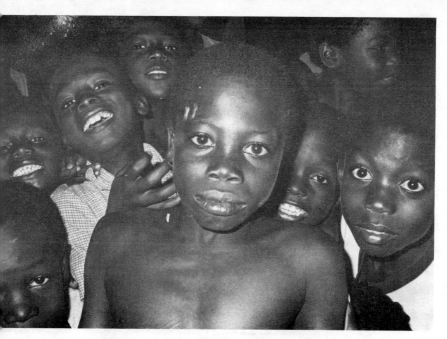

. These Garifuna children represent just one of the unreached people groups now being reached by the *JESUS* film. More than 160 mission groups are now using the film to establish new churches.

. Wycliffe translator, Lillian Howland, completed the Garifuna New Testament in 1984 after 30 years of work. A few months later she translated the script for the *JESUS* film in Garifuna.

11. Baptist missionary, David Dickson, sets up the portable screen in a Honduran fishing village for the premiere showing of the Garifuna translation. On the left is Robert Foree, Texas businessman who helped to finance the translation.

12. This film team in Sri Lanka rides local buses between villages.

13. The only way to reach some remote villages in Indonesia is by boat.

14. In India the only transportation available in some villages is foot power.

15. One Colombia film team uses pack mules and horses for showings in the mountains.

. Before every film showing, counselors are trained to help follow up those who express interest at the conclusion of the film.

. This Masai warrior chief has helped thousands to find Christ through film showings in southern Kenya.

18. Samburu warriors in northern Kenya also respond to the film.

19. In Kinshasa, Zaire, 11,500 watch the film. More than 1,000 expressed a desire to receive Chris

21. Crowds in India sometimes number more than 20,000.

...creens are not always fancy. Some are
mple bedsheets tacked to wooden poles.

23. Many respond to the invitation at the end of
the film. Maureen Smith, a Canadian staff
member, reads through the Four Spiritual
Laws in Portuguese with interested Brazilians.

24. In Africa, those interested in accepting Jesus as their Savior are asked to come to the light. Non-literate counselors are able to explain the gospel again by means of a picture-book flipchart.

25. Scripture portions are provided for these new believers in Mexico by a Canadian student involved in a summer project.

26. The nomadic Masai of Kenya meet und trees.

. The *JESUS* film on national TV in
Cyprus — subtitled in Greek.

28. The Classic Cinema in Westcliff, England, was
filled for weeks during the showings of *JESUS*.

This church in Pamongan, Indonesia, has grown to 200 in just one year.
All are former Muslims.

30. This Here's Life Training Center in Indonesia helps prepare pastors and leaders for the thousands of Home Bible Fellowships which are being started as a result of the film showings.

31. In the last five years in Thailand, 4,251 Home Bible Fellowships have formed, plus 481 churches.

32. One theater in Uganda which was constr with banana leaves so film showings cou be done during the day. This pastor saw church grow from 30 to more than 600 one year from the showings of the film.

33. The Jesus Project goal is to dub the film into the 271 languages which have more than a million speakers each.

34. Pierce Barnes demonstrates new portable equipment that permits high quality dubbing of languages in the most remote corners of the world.

35. Careful editing by Pierce Barnes and Tom Dennen in our master studio allows Jesus to speak Bengali, Swahili and Aztec.

36. Canadian students conducted 462 showings along the Amazon River in Brazil. More than 16,000 indicated decisions for Christ and 577 follow-up groups were established.

37. Some are dedicated to taking the film to the lepers in India.

38. Unreached peoples. There are thousands of people groups like the Tarahumara Indians that have yet to be reached.

39. The joy on Peter's face is evident during the triumphal entry of Jesus into Jerusalem.

40. The suffering of Jesus as He is nailed to the cross.

41. There is great excitement when this scene is shown in fishing villages throughout the world.

CHAPTER THIRTEEN
A TIME TO REAP

The town of Whitefield, India, lies just outside of Bangalore. On a hot and humid Saturday afternoon I walked along the dusty roads to the humble home of the Reverend S. Dinakaran, the Nazarene pastor mentioned earlier. The once tidy little colony around me was built more than a hundred years ago by the British as an exclusive housing area, but with the passing of British colonialism the rich estates have become little more than the wreckage of a bygone era.

A stately old town square is crowded now with a jumble of makeshift stalls set up in dusty spaces. The once regal whitewashed pillars of the general store are flaking and encrusted with the stain and disrepair of years of neglect, and in their shadow leathery-skinned women in ragged clothing sell fruit and vegetables to anyone who can buy. Gaunt, hollow-eyed old men sit cross-legged in the dirt holding out coconuts to passersby, while goats and dogs vie with the flies for the garbage rotting at their feet. And everywhere the children play, barefoot and dirty, unconscious of the stench rising from the streets around them.

In the midst of it all are the ever present signs of man's eternal search for God. Hindu women, the marks of their caste on their foreheads, enter an ancient temple across from the market; Muslim women, covered from head to toe in garments of black, bargain with the vendors for what they need; and the seller in a shaded stall offers pictures and the literature of the Sathya Sai Baba.

But the smiling reverend is not discouraged. "What God is doing here," he said, "is a miracle!" The whiteness of his teeth struck a contrast with his smooth, brown skin and his black eyes flashed with excitement. "Let me tell you how the *JESUS* film has helped us here.

"Many missionaries have ministered in Whitefield long years with no results, only discouragement and Satanic oppression. Walter Cowen and his wife came from North America and became so disheartened that they deserted their faith and gave all they had to Sai Baba.

"Those few who have dared to follow Christ were openly persecuted by others. One radical Hindu group entered a home where several Christians had gathered, beat them severely and told them they could no longer meet to worship Christ. In spite of it all, God is in control.

"One day I heard about the *JESUS* film and the training in evangelism that Campus Crusade provides. I remember praying earnestly one night that somehow God would let us use this film; I asked Him for ten showings in our area. *The very next day God sent Charlie Abro from India Campus Crusade to my house.* He explained that he was training film team workers to go into north India and he wondered if I would like to use them for the next forty days!"

He laughed out loud, remembering the excitement of God's answer to his prayer. "I can't tell you how wonderful it was, Paul. Hundreds responded to the message."

"How many people are in this area?" I asked. He took me to a hand-drawn map tacked on the wall. At the top he had written in large letters: "Goal for Evangelization and Church Planting." He tapped the center of the map with his finger. "In about five square kilometers there are thirty villages and thirty-three thousand people. But you know, during the forty days that the film teams were here we reached every one of the thirty targeted villages and between a thousand and fifteen hundred came to each showing. Fifteen to twenty in each village accepted Christ as we followed up."

The reverend was completely absorbed in his ministry. It showed all over him as he talked with great animation of what the Lord was doing in Whitefield. He hardly noticed a small bird that slipped through a space below the eaves of the roof and flew around the room. She settled in a corner above us to add twigs to a nest she was building in the rafters.

The reverend's living room was nothing more than a small cube furnished with two old chairs, a cabinet overflowing with follow-up literature and stacks of New Testaments, a few books, and room to park his motorcycle. I could not help but wonder how many others would even consider living as simply as he did, yet to him to be part of evangelizing Whitefield was a God-given privilege that he loved.

"How many of the thirty-three thousand have seen the film, Reverend?"

He smiled proudly. "All of them have seen it at least once. So far, twenty-three thousand have seen it twice."

"Tell me about the results."

"We have four churches now and at least twenty-five

people in each have been baptized and become members. Many more attend each week who have received Christ, but you must understand that in this Hindu culture baptism often results in persecution.

"Anyone may attend the church but we require baptism for membership and we don't baptize new believers until we are certain they have counted the cost of their new commitment and really understand what it could mean to them personally. It's not unusual for a new believer converted from Hinduism to be beaten severely by his own family. Some have had their clothing burned and been thrown out of their homes. Disowned.

"But people keep coming. Besides the four new churches we also have five new prayer cells with twenty to twenty-five members in each. We are praying these will also become churches, but we need more pastors first."

How different from in America where we so often feel the need to court and entertain our church members to keep them coming. Here in India, in the face of persecution and hardship, this incredible brother is pastoring four churches and leading five prayer cells. What just a little help would mean to him!

Miracles happen every day in places like Whitefield. As the reverend went from house to house distributing invitations to a film showing he asked a woman to come. She pointed to her daughter who was lying in the dirt, her body contorted with the pain of dysentery. "I cannot come," said the worried mother. "My daughter is too ill. She has been like this for days."

"Would you come if your daughter were well?" he asked. The woman said she would, and the reverend prayed, asking in the name of Jesus that the child be healed. As they watched, the pain left the child's body and she stood to her feet, strong and well, the dysentery gone. That night the mother came to the showing as she had promised, and she brought thirty friends and relatives. Nearly all of them are now believers.

In another village Dinakaran and his team were badly beaten by Hindu leaders for starting a worship service. When they told the commissioner of police what had happened to them, the stern-faced official leveled his gaze at the reverend. "Are you trying to convert people to another religion?" he demanded. "That is against the law!"

"I know that, sir," Dinakaran replied. "We are not trying to convert anyone to a new religion. Our only interest is in seeing people's lives changed, and no one but God can do that." The commissioner thought a moment, then assigned his staff to protect the film team whenever they held meetings.

Last year the largest crowd ever to meet in Whitefield Centre gathered to celebrate Thanksgiving. More than four thousand people met for worship and prayer — the result of the faithfulness, fasting and prayers of a handful of people who had come to love Jesus, the One they met through a film.

* * *

Elsewhere in India the film was drawing crowds far beyond what anyone could have predicted. In the Maharashtra city of Ahmadnagar, more than twenty thousand viewed the first showing. In an Andra Pradesh village nine thousand people came, forcing the cancellation of other movies playing in nearby theaters. In yet another Indian village the film was shown to twelve thousand at a Hindu festival *in the temple*.

Electricity is often a problem in these provinces, with the power not coming on when it is expected. Still the crowds wait patiently sometimes until 2:00 or 3:00 in the morning for the film to begin. And it is not unusual for audiences to ask to see the film again as soon as it has ended. On one occasion a crowd sat on the ground all night to see *JESUS* three consecutive times.

The film is often well received when other evangelistic methods are not. In a village in Karnataka a gospel team trying to conduct open air meetings was driven away as nationals threatened to burn their van and literature. The film team arrived the next day and was given immediate permission to show the picture. More than five thousand people came to see *JESUS* and asked the team afterward to take it to other nearby villages.

In a city not far from there, a team was showing the film outdoors. Officials had given permission to block traffic for the evening, but people complained that they could not see the screen because of the glare of the street lights. The Hindu leaders of the village called a lineman to switch the lights off until they had seen the film. Ten thousand watched that showing!

In another village it seemed that there would be no showing of *JESUS*. The only source of power was in the Temple of Hunan, the monkey god where an "eternal" light burns before the idol and is never allowed to go out. There was no way to power the projector, but the Hindu priest wanted to see the film so he took it upon himself to unplug the "eternal" light and connect the film team's equipment in its place for the showing. More than two thousand people watched the picture with the priest.

CHAPTER FOURTEEN
SOME
DIFFICULT PLACES

By early evening, in a vacant lot in Usulatan, El Salvador, Pablo and his film team were finishing the final preparations for the showing of *JESUS* that night. Several hundred people had already gathered and others were coming down the dusty roads alone or in small groups. They stood or sat together in nervous clusters, involved in a hushed chatter but not relaxing.

And then they heard it: the sound of an approaching plane. A common enough occurrence, but to these people there was a difference. They had learned to listen for and identify the sounds of an impending attack. It was part of the skill needed to stay alive in El Salvador now.

The aircraft strained as it climbed into the sky above them. It was the first of the signs — and all they needed to hear. Everyone ran from the vacant lot to find cover. Overhead the plane seemed to stall, then suddenly it dropped toward the earth, broadcasting a chilling scream as it fell toward its target.

Within seconds no one on the ground was in sight. Everyone was hidden, trembling, waiting inside the surrounding adobe huts, which provided little more than the feeling of protection. The plane roared low, flying a line just across the street from the lot where the movie screen still stood. The pilot strafed a row of red tile roofs with machine gun fire and a swarm of frightened young men with M-16s slung over their shoulders bolted from the doors and windows to take cover in the denseness of the surrounding trees.

No one moved for several minutes; they were waiting to see if the plane would make another attach on the village. Pablo lay in his shelter, telling God of the disappointment he felt that no one would come to the showing of the film tonight. They would have to wrap up the equipment and try again the next night.

When it seemed safe enough to come out, he stood to his feet — and was surprised to see what was happening. Several of the villagers were already making their way back into the lot and settling down, waiting for the picture. Pablo couldn't help grinning. There was a showing that night with over five hundred brave souls coming back into the open to watch.

* * *

El Salvadorans are responding to the film in surprisingly large numbers. During one week of some of the fiercest fighting, the film was shown in Santa Telca, a city of fifty-two thousand. Some twenty-three thousand people came and more than fifty-six hundred made decisions to receive Christ.

High school and college students have volunteered to show the film across the war-torn Central American republic of 4.5 million people. The once dynamic economy has been stifled and some forty thousand have been reported killed by the guns of extremist "death squads." Yet, in one week alone, more than sixty-five thousand from five cities saw *JESUS*. They have come in crowds ranging from five hundred to three thousand depending on the safety of the area, and 10 percent have indicated decisions for Christ.

* * *

In Sonsonate, El Salvador, a crowd of three thousand was viewing the film when a band of soldiers marched into the area. They asked who was in charge, and Andres, the film team leader, stepped forward. Without further question or explanation Andres was taken into custody and marched away. The bewildered audience waited. The film team prayed.

Andres was taken to the private quarters of the local military commander and questioned. Why had so many people been gathered together in one place? What was the purpose? In simple terms Andres explained the gospel to him and the commander listened thoughtfully. "I want to see this film for myself," he said.

Some time after his arrest, Andres returned to the location of the showing. There, waiting patiently, was the crowd of three thousand. Andres walked to the back of the group, rolled the film back to the beginning and started the projector again. This time, however, the audience had increased by fifty officers and two hundred soldiers.

* * *

In the pueblo Santa Maria Ostuma, nearly half the town turned out for the first showing. Church members participated in personal evangelism during the day, and the film was shown at night. In four showings, six thousand people saw the film with five hundred indicating a decision for Christ.

Adonai Leiva, Campus Crusade director for the country,

says, "We have claimed Isaiah 9:1 for El Salvador: 'There will be no more gloom for those who were in distress' " (New International Version). By the end of 1988, the film had been seen by more than 1,100,000 El Salvadorans.

* * *

The angry crowd of women marched straight through the streets of Managua, Nicaragua, and right up to Felipe Gonzales.

"How dare you shame the name of Jesus!" the leader shouted into his face.

Felipe was at a total loss. "But," he stammered, "I love Jesus!"

The woman narrowed her eyes. "Then why have you made a film that disgraces Him, uh? Tell me that, Felipe Gonzales. You are full of disrespect for God!"

"No, no," he said. "It is a good film — a film that teaches of the goodness of God."

"Then why does our government not recommend it for our children to see?" someone in the crowd shouted. It took a while to calm the women down and to explain that Nicaraguan officials thought the picture could be "too emotion-provoking for children." They seemed less angry, but they were not convinced.

"Then come, see for yourselves," he said. He held the door as they filed into the little Managuan theater. Two hours later the spokeswoman had prayed to receive the Christ of the JESUS film she had objected to. As she spoke with the young Campus Crusade staff member who had led her to Christ, she agreed to organize a showing in her own area of the city.

A few days later the woman and her new Christian

friend, the staff member, entered the office of the municipal president of her area. "I don't know how to explain these things very well yet," she said to the man behind the desk. "All I know is that I have received Christ into my life. My friend is going to tell you how you can receive Him in your life too." She leveled her gaze at the man. "I want you to receive Him," she said, "and then I want you to give us permission to show the *JESUS* film here."

Obediently the man listened, fascinated by what the staff woman had to say. When she finished the official hungrily opened his heart to Christ . . . and arranged a showing of the film as he had been asked.

* * *

Separate permission must be granted for each barrio (neighborhood) showing, and as the meetings for these permits have proceeded, staff members have found themselves praying with countless city officials who desired to accept Christ. As a result, most of Managua's barrios have had at least one *JESUS* showing. During a five-month span in 1983, some ninety-two thousand Nicaraguans crowded churches, theaters and baseball fields to see *JESUS*.

Nicaraguans are incensed by the revolutionary government's subtle and overt attempts to suppress their centuries-old religious pride. Many of the people have begun manifesting an increasing spiritual fervor, as the angry woman of Managua did.

Deprival of essentials like oil, bread and soap, and the constant threat of war have forced these people to look beyond human provision. There has been an upsurge of interest in the things of God, and *JESUS* has provided thousands with the answers they are seeking.

At one showing held in a Managua baseball field, the

film team asked those who had received Christ to walk to a nearby church to receive some free literature. Nine hundred people crowded into the church leaving many outside, waiting.

The following week staff members met at the same church with new believers to offer further instruction in their faith. Then the staff went into the surrounding barrios to share their faith. Many of the new converts went along for the first time.

"The best part about this," Felipe said later, "is the excitement they have about Jesus. One young man, a Christian for only a week, came back from the barrios bursting with news. Five people had received Christ that afternoon because he had shared his faith."

On October 31, 1985, the official "JESUS" film showings in Nicaragua came to an end. Sandinista officials confiscated all of the "JESUS" films and equipment. Several of the staff were stripped, beaten, and pistol-whipped. Our director was interrogated for three days and finally forced to leave the country. But by the time he left, several million had seen the film and many hundreds of thousands had responded to the message.

CHAPTER FIFTEEN
BREAKING
ALL THE BARRIERS

It was a cold and rainy afternoon when we arrived at the parish in southern Poland. Inside the stone building more than two hundred young people were training to become Bible study leaders for new Christians, part of the follow-up for the showings of *JESUS*. Father John welcomed us warmly and ushered us inside out of the cold.

Most of the films we shipped to Poland are used by those involved in OAZA, a liturgical reform movement started within the Catholic church. It has become increasingly evangelistic in its thrust. As a young college girl interpreted, I asked Father John what their plans were.

"To show the film in all the parishes in Poland," he said. He smiled at the thought. "You know, of course, 98 percent of Poland is Catholic, but many are Catholic only by culture. They do not have a personal faith. We want to use the film to change that, you see, and so we prepare for the follow-up. We must have the Bible study."

"Do the people of your parish have Bibles?" I asked.

"Very few — 10 percent or less." He led me up a narrow staircase to a workroom in the attic. "Here I am

making Bible study courses," he said proudly. He handed
me several ditto sheets. They were barely legible. He
shrugged, "It is the best this old machine can do. We so
desperately need an off-set press. Oh, what I could do
with that!"

"Do the authorities care that you do this?"

"Well, they're not so much in favor." He seemed
uneasy; then he shrugged slightly and said, "But somehow
we must help people to know the Bible, so we train study
leaders, schedule one or two showings of the film for the
parish, then sign up those who are interested in a four-week
Bible study." Later I discovered that each of the four
weeks focuses on one of the four spiritual laws.

Father John had asked me to speak to the young
people who were training as leaders. "Tell them what is
happening in other parts of the world," he said. "We feel
so isolated here. We need to know what God is doing in
other places."

The mass began and I was surrounded with young
voices raised in praise to God. Familiar melodies were
like old friends and the presence of the Lord warmed us
all in that chilly sanctuary.

Sharing with these Polish believers was a special
blessing for me. They were openly stirred with stories of
Muslims in Asia, secular humanists in Western Europe
and tribal peoples in Africa all coming to Christ. And as
my interpreter translated each phrase, I saw a radiance
come to the young faces looking back at me. They were
being encouraged, reminded that they were not a struggling
minority but part of a worldwide family lifting up Jesus
as Lord. Tears overflowed from hearts grateful to hear
what God was doing through brothers and sisters around
the world.

After Father John had led communion he dismissed the mass and directed the crowd to break into small discussion groups. Our interpreter led us to several groups to listen in.

One group was talking with a young college girl, earnestly trying to share their faith in a way that she would respond to. A young man leaned toward her and said, "But look into our eyes. Surely you can tell that we have the truth. Jesus is the truth."

"I looked into the eyes of an old man in the park yesterday," she answered. "I think he had the truth too. I believe we're all part of God and God is a part of each of us, and of everything in nature." She sounded like an art or philosophy major from Cal Berkeley.

With my interpreter's help I asked if the young woman would mind answering a few questions for me. She agreed.

"If there really is a God," I said, "and you could know Him personally, would you want to?"

"Yes," she said. "I really would."

"If the way to know God is to accept Jesus as payment for your sin, and invite Him into your life, would you be willing to do that?"

She thought for a moment, then said softly, "Yes."

I glanced at the group. The openness and love I saw in them rebuked and humbled me. There were tears in their eyes as they prayed for this one whom they loved. I could not recall the last time I had wept with the desire for another's faith. Their young hearts were filled with love for their friend and with prayers that she would choose to believe in the Lord they loved so much.

I looked back with new vision at the young woman

answering my questions. "Would you like me to lead you in a prayer so that you can invite Jesus to become your personal Savior?"

"Yes," she said, and there in that circle of believers, in a language I could not understand, phrase by translated phrase, another child entered the kingdom. We said "Amen" and her friends rushed to her, hugging her, weeping together with genuine joy.

By 1988, despite martial law, food shortages and tremendous political turmoil, more than seven million people throughout Poland had seen *JESUS*. It has been shown during lunch hours in many factories of Gdansk where the Solidarity movement began. We are grateful to the authorities who permitted these showings.

* * *

We should not have been surprised — after all, God is the God of the impossible — but when the Muslim censor board in Iran cleared the film, it seemed incredible. The country that will not permit entry to a book with the word "God" in the title, had okayed *JESUS* to be shown.

The Vatican Ambassador opened the premier showing for four hundred people, and almost half those present received Christ at the end.

On the road to Damascus in Syria four thousand of the seven thousand citizens of Homs attended the showing.

One of the hottest rental items in the twenty-six video stores in the tiny island nation of Bahrain in the Persian Gulf, is the Arabic version of *JESUS*. Poorer people pool their resources and rent a large-screen television, *JESUS*, and four or five other pictures for the weekend. Wealthy old sheiks rent it for their own players. Thousands have heard and seen the message of love in Bahrain.

On the other end of the world, the film shows in East Germany where the government has permitted the YMCA to import five prints in German. During the first six months it was shown to more than 250,000 people.

In Burma a team showed *JESUS* at a Buddhist monastery. At the conclusion the abbot said, "You must tell all the people of Rangoon and Mandalay that new life can be found in Jesus!" They then invited the team to show the film again at the ordination of a new Catholic bishop. Officials estimated the crowd in attendance to be nearly thirty thousand.

An underground cave in Egypt became the theater for *JESUS* during the celebration of the annual Feast of the Virgin. Thirty-three thousand could be seated and showings were kept running twenty-four hours a day for nearly two weeks. Five-hundred thousand heard the gospel!

In the Muslim dominated country of Pakistan there is great interest in the gospel. During a seven-month period more than three-hundred thousand people saw *JESUS* in eight areas. Over ninety-four thousand indicated decisions to receive Christ, and stories keep filtering back to us from Pakistan.

In upper Sind thirty "highwaymen" accepted Christ after seeing the film and asked to be baptized.

The film was shown in the national center of the central government of Sargodba, the first Christian program in history.

The Muslim staff in Purjah's Information Department set up showings of the film in two churches and *provided their own projector and screen.*

The room was still dark after the showing of *JESUS* in the Leiah district, and a Muslim man could not escape the conviction building in his heart. With tears streaming down his face, he stood to his feet in the crowd and cried out to God for forgiveness.

* * *

For nearly four years Vek Huong Taing, Campus Crusade's leader in Phnom Penh, had been missing without a trace. Then he was discovered in the Taphraya refugee camp in Thailand, just north of Aranyaprathet and one mile from the Cambodian border. He and 140,000 other forgotten people were jammed into makeshift bamboo huts, grateful for a cup of rice twice a day and a tin of sardines once a week.

Living conditions were unbelievable. People were reduced to the level of animals, made to work at hard labor, deprived of the smallest pleasures, such as clean water and a chance to bathe. Sickness flourished, spirits weakened, feeling people became numb to the pain they could not escape.

Through a series of diplomatic miracles, Taing was allowed to come to the United States with his wife and son. But behind him, in the squalor and stench of that fearful place of pity, he left thirty relatives, three of them tiny, newborn babies. A few months later Bill Bright and I returned to the camp carrying a few cloth diapers and a copy of the *JESUS* film dubbed into Cambodian by Taing and other refugees in America.

By the time Bill and I arrived there was a large bamboo church in Khaoidong. It had been started a few months before by the first Christians refugees relocated here. Now they numbered eight thousand, and met in hundreds of home churches throughout the camp.

They were open about their meetings and met with permission, but it remained dangerous to name the name of Christ. Persecution was common and cruel. Severe beatings were widespread, and one believer had been thrown into boiling water, almost costing his life.

In cooperation with Food-for-the-Hungry, Campus Center refugee coordinator, Paul Utley, secured permission for the *JESUS* film to be shown by the pastor of the bamboo hut church. Working around the early evening curfew and other intrinsic problems, the believers began showing the film every day after we left.

One year later I returned to the camp and could not believe what I saw. The face of the grounds was not the same. Eighty thousand refugees had been relocated, and those who remained had begun to take hopeful pride in themselves and their meager surroundings. Gardens had been planted, and a return of caring for the welfare of others flourished as well.

The Cambodian pastor beamed. "It is because of the film," he said. "We showed it every day until our six-month permit ran out, but by then we did not mind. Everyone in camp saw the film; many saw it over and over. Thousands came to Christ through *JESUS* and lives changed. You can see it all around you." Tears filled his coal-black eyes. "Thank you for the film. It gave us back the source of life."

* * *

A few months ago I was in Washington, D.C., on business, and I got to talking to the Cambodian maid who cleaned my hotel room. Before long I discovered she was a Christian too.

"How long have you been a Christian?" I asked.

She smiled broadly and in her broken English said, "More than one year."

"Where did you hear about Jesus?"

"In a refugee camp in Thailand," she said. "I saw a film called *JESUS*."

CHAPTER SIXTEEN
THEY PAY A PRICE

They were two days behind schedule because of the flood. Unseasonal rains had swelled the rivers and the film team waited to transport their equipment through the jungle-like terrain. They were anxious to reach their destination, the village on the other side of the swollen river.

Finally, a crossing was possible. As dawn was breaking the team members loaded the thirty-pound projector, a sixty-pound generator, the four-reel film weighing fifteen pounds, and an assortment of cords, screens, voltage regulators, portable screen pieces, petrol cans and luggage back onto the cart behind a pair of water buffalo that had been yoked together and was waiting.

They had planned well; the river crossing was uneventful. Soon they were following the trail that ran beside the river and that would take them to their village. Late that afternoon they stood in the spot where the showing was scheduled. The river had swept it clean. Nothing remained but silt, a few felled trees and boggy mud up to their ankles.

They looked around them in disbelief. This was the place all right. They had been here just a few weeks

before to make arrangements to bring the film in. And
now they stood in the center of what used to be a thriving
village. Every hut and stand had been swept away by the
flood. There was no village. There was no one left to see
the film.

Tired and disappointed, they looked at each other — so
much work for nothing. With a sigh they turned the weary
buffalo toward home and started the long trip back.

* * *

Each summer thousands of students and lay people
raise the money to cover their expenses and travel to Asia,
Africa, and Latin America on film teams. They give up
comfortable beds to sleep in hammocks on an Amazon
river boat, a straw mat beside a Philippine rice paddy, or
a sleeping bag on the floor of an African mud hut.

Their schedule is demanding, the work is hard and
the difficulties endless. For every showing in every village,
they must locate a place to stay and a way to feed
themselves, and they must adapt to diets that are strange
to them. In most places they battle language barriers,
unable to express even the simplest thought without an
interpreter. There are cultural barriers that confront them,
and the threat — and reality — of diarrhea, dysentery and
malaria.

In every new place they must establish hearings with
town officials and gain permission to show the film; then
they have to involve local churches, train counselors, and
do personal evangelism. In many places religious prejudice
precedes them, creating situations of very real danger, and
in other places national unrest and war threaten their very
lives.

Under unpredictable and sometimes frightening circumstances, they show the film, guide non-believers to

new relationships with Christ, and begin discipleship groups that continue in local churches long after the team has returned home. Because of the continuous strain placed on team members, there is time set aside daily for personal quiet times with the Lord, Bible study, and team prayer. Every week or two they have a few days for rest, recreation and spiritual restoration. Team members testify to incredible personal growth, and to learning new lessons in spiritual values.

Every day teams around the world are called upon to bring their equipment into remote locations and show the *JESUS* film to those who wait for the message. Of the hundreds of teams in eighty-five countries, less than fifty have the luxury of using a jeep or an all-terrain vehicle to haul necessities. The rest make do with what they can find.

Gear has been transported in every conceivable way. In the Pacific Islands and Indonesia the most practical method is boat or canoe. Wherever possible, buses are used, but where nothing else is available animal-drawn carts and wagons are brought into play. In many countries the water buffalo is a common source of "power" for this mode of transportation.

Still there remain locations where only one form of transportation is truly practical: good old manpower. In these places film team members carry their paraphernalia by hand, sometimes for miles.

A most unusual episode occurred in Burma when the film was scheduled to be shown in the remote village of Hsanguang. Village officials sent word to Campus Crusade of their desire to see the film, and requested that it be brought in during their harvest festival.

Hsanguang, located high in the mountains and nestled

beneath lush, tropical vegetation, is nearly inaccessible and it seemed the only possible way to get the equipment in was by helicopter. Since our teams run on tight budgets, especially in the jungle, a helicopter shuttle was eliminated as a possibility because of the expense. Sadly, the team sent word back to the village that they could not come because of transportation limitations.

The next day, as one young team member stood under a tree finishing his morning coffee, something appeared that he never expected to see. There in the clearing before him, stood two gigantic elephants and a smiling messenger. "The elephants have come to take you over the mountain," the little man said. The team member set his coffee down and went to get the others.

Carefully they packed the pachyderms with everything they would need, climbed aboard and lumbered off over the mountain. Results? Sixty-five hundred people witnessed the film during the festival, and one hundred forty-one claimed Christ as their Lord and Savior. And none of it would have happened without the elephants God sent.

Surprises, danger and hardship remain, but the life of a *JESUS* film team member is seldom dull. From every kind of background, every walk of life — Campus Crusade staff members, church members, college students, laypersons and nationals — these are people with a vision of reaching the lost for Christ, *and they are doing something about it!*

* * *

In Thailand a team supervisor had just finished threading the film into the projector when he felt the cold steel of a gun barrel pressed against the back of his head. The gunman demanded that the team leave the area. Frozen with fear, no one moved.

"I am not afraid to die for Jesus," the supervisor said.

"If I were afraid to die, I would not be here."

The gunman looked at him for a moment, then pocketed his gun and left. The film showing went on as scheduled.

At another outdoor showing in Thailand a man tried to hit team members with stones he lobbed from a catapult. Instead, he hit a woman in the audience . . . she turned out to be his own mother.

Charlie Abro, coordinator for *JESUS* in India, says, "Every film team in India has been beaten and stoned. We don't even think about it anymore. Everyone has problems to face; this is just one of ours."

Bandits roam and plunder in large sections of India. Many are better armed than the sprinkling of police authority. In one small village the film was just about to begin when runners breathlessly warned of bandits on their way to attack.

Frightened villagers fled and when the bandits arrived only the team remained with their equipment. Most Indians love movies, and bandits are no exception. The showing that night was an exclusive screening for bandits only. Several received Christ, and the village was spared.

On several occasions, radical Muslim zealots in Indonesia have thrown team members to the ground and burned them on the face with cigarettes.

In the north of Celebes, Franky Devgah, a Campus Crusade staff member, made his second follow-up visit to a home in the capital city of Menudo. His companion that warm, humid night was a young Muslim convert called Alwi. They began to speak to a group of twenty or so, three of whom were angry Muslim radicals.

Franky spoke to the group for half an hour, then someone offered him a cup of tea. Grateful for the refreshment, Franky swallowed some of the tea, then stopped. It felt like pins were running down his throat and suddenly his stomach was filled with knife-like pain.

Quickly he made his apologies and left, ran to a small church nearby and pounded on the pastor's door. He begged him for canned milk which he gulped directly from the can. He vomited a green-colored fluid — proof that he had swallowed strychnine, a deadly poison.

Unaware of what had happened to Franky, Alwi drank his tea and soon came running to the church, also in need of help. Franky and the pastor made him drink canned milk too, then both men were taken to the hospital for further care.

The next week they were back at the same home in Menudo where they told the astonished group, "We came to tell you we have forgiven you in the name of Jesus." That discipling group has doubled.

On entering a small village in East Asia, a film team was stoned by an angry mob that gathered to keep them out. Undaunted, they moved on to the next village, where they were met by a Hindu priest.

He listened as they shared the gospel with him, then eagerly received Christ. When they left,he insisted on traveling with them, at least to the next village a few miles down the road.

When they got there, the skeptical villagers watched the film team through narrowed eyes. Soon they, too, were picking up stones from the ground and throwing them at the team.

Standing to his full height in the center of the crowd, the priest was a fearful sight in his flowing sacred robes. His face was flushed with anger, though his position was enough to strike terror into the hearts of every villager there.

In a booming voice he shouted, "Why are you doing this? These Christians have not come to harm you! They bring good news!"

Confused and frightened, the people backed away. Why was this honored Hindu priest defending Christians?

With anger flashing in his eyes, the priest tore his holy robes off his body and flung them to the ground. The people gasped in disbelief, and as they watched, he set the sacred garments on fire, an act which could have cost him his life.

A dramatic hush fell over everyone as each man and woman weighed within themselves what they had seen and heard. The team marveled at the boldness of this brand new believer. It seemed like something that would have happened in the Book of Acts.

One by one the villagers dropped the rocks they held, and in shy curiosity, gathered around to find out what was happening. The team set up the film and the entire village watched *JESUS* that night, hearing the gospel for the first time in their lives.

Rebel extremists in the Philippines threw a bomb into a showing, but miraculously, no one was killed. The injured were taken for help and within an hour the film was restarted, this time to a larger crowd than before.

It is against the law in Nepal to change from the religion of your father, but in the past few years thousands have seen the *JESUS* film and hundreds of new believers have been baptized. At various times, as many as fifty or sixty new believers have been in jail at one time for changing their faith. Currently, some of the key evangelical leaders there face sentences of up to five years for preaching the gospel. The price is high.

In a small tin-roofed shack in northern Kenya, two American college students lay shivering on mats on a concrete floor. The temperature outside was over a hundred degrees, but despite the heat and unbearable humidity their bodies were chilled with the fever of malaria.

Several teams in different parts of the world have contracted malaria and other sicknesses, yet God has provided the strength to recover and to continue performing the taxing responsibilities that fall to them.

A visitor to that shack in Kenya commented that it seemed like these young people were paying an awfully high price for the cause of the gospel.

The answer was simple for one member of the team. "Sir," he said to the visitor, "to bring the message to those who have never heard, there is no price too high to pay."

CHAPTER SEVENTEEN
SUMMER SAFARI

Judy George reviewed the contents of her backpack one more time for good measure: two changes of clothes, bandages for blisters, toothbrush, hairbrush, shampoo, Bible, four pairs of socks . . . It didn't seem like much, especially when it was going to have to last a couple of months in the mountainous terrain where they were going, but that was it. There just would not be room for anything else. Talk about "traveling light . . ."

That feeling surged within her again, that thrill of adventure she got every time she remembered where she really was, what she was doing with her life. Judy George was in the Philippines, taking the gospel to people who had never heard the name of Jesus! It seemed too incredible to believe, even after all the training and the months of service here in Luzon as a health worker.

She could have chosen to walk into some safe nursing job back in Pocatello, Idaho, but what for? Here, she was confronted daily with the fact that she was affecting lives for eternity. She smiled to herself and slung her bulging backpack over her slender shoulder. She was ready to go wherever the Lord took her and the team. Ready and eager!

Food was not a problem. They were taking none because there was no room, and they could feed themselves along the way. But there was equipment to take, and it was evenly distributed among the four team members: one filmstrip projector, film strips and literature, and one car battery that was going to have to be carried the whole way, but they would manage. They always did.

The first leg of the journey was relatively easy, getting from the city out to the rural sections and beginning the climb toward the mountains. The surrounding country was beautiful and Judy drank it all in: the tropical vegetation, the wonderful open skies overhead, the incredible cloud formations that pushed along ahead of the wind.

It was a beautiful day, too nice to let the heat and humidity become a problem even if it was suffocating. Besides, Judy and the other members of the team were almost used to it. The sudden rains and constant humidity kept everything green and lush and productive. In this section of the country, miles and miles of terraced rice fields covered the face of the mountain. Farmers had dug levees to provide the standing water needed to plant and raise their crops.

The patterned mountains were a beautiful sight but climbing the steep hills around them was not easy. Some of it was almost straight up, and the footing was loose and slippery. Judy could not help but notice that her feet were already blistered and becoming more tender by the minute. They would have to toughen up or it would, indeed, be a long summer.

She carefully picked her footing along the dike between the terraces, but at one spot the ground was softer than she had guessed and she slipped off the edge into the rice paddy. Before she knew what was happening she was standing waist deep in water, her jeans and shoes and socks submerged somewhere beneath the soggy surface. A little embarrassed, but noticeably cooler, she scrambled back up the embankment to the top of the levee.

It was good for a laugh and a lot of friendly teasing but the pretty, lean brunette was good-natured. She could afford to be — she figured she would get her chance to even the score before long. It was not more than a few minutes later when one of the young men in the party lost his footing and slid down the slippery face of the mountain a hundred feet or so, hollering all the way.

Arriving at a village meant there was work to be done. Permission was always the first concern, to find officials and obtain their O.K. to show the filmstrip and talk to the villagers about the gospel. Then they looked for food and a place to sleep.

The first few weeks had the flavor of a camping trip for Judy, but that soon wore off into the realization that this was just plain, hard living. Diet consisted of rice and beans, sometimes canned sardines or something that the villagers would give or sell to them, like cooking bananas. Judy ate seven one day because there was nothing else.

Occasionally they stayed in the home of a village Christian, but for the most part they slept in empty school buildings. It was not unusual for them to be unable to locate a place to stay until well after dark, and more nights than not they ended up sleeping in a tin-roofed shack with no electricity, in the company of large and curious rats, and with no toilet. When a trip to the "bush toilet" was necessary, they took two sticks along to hit together to keep the pigs from following them.

Many nights Judy George collapsed on her makeshift bed, so exhausted she could hardly move. The blisters on her feet were sore and bleeding, and the thought of walking another three or four hours the next day brought tears to her eyes.

"Lord," she whispered, "I don't mean to be a complainer, it's just that my feet hurt so bad tonight, and I'm so tired, and I'm sick of eating bananas. I'd give anything for a long hot shower and a chance to wash my hair in water that *isn't* downstream from men washing their water buffalo and their trucks!"

But as she lay there in the darkness she would remember the faces of the mountain people she had talked with and touched that day, and the children, who gathered around her, touching her light skin and talking among themselves, so fascinated by her height and the fact that her hair was not ebony like theirs.

She thought about the people. So poor. So desperately in need of Jesus. Beautiful mountain faces. Open hearts, hungry for the gospel of love. She wished every day that she could speak their language and didn't have to rely on interpreters to say what she felt. It was reaching these people that made it worth it all. She would do it all again if it meant one person would find Christ.

Judy would sigh and close her eyes, now heavy with sleep. "Lord," she would say, "give me a better attitude about the tough stuff we face. I want to count for You, so use me, Lord; just use me up if You need to."

There were places where anti-government guerrillas would hide and nights when the team wondered if they would live to see morning. But it was in those places, facing those situations that Judy and the others learned that security had nothing to do with where a person is, or what his position might be, or what he owns, but only in a real relationship with the Lord. Nothing on earth could threaten that security.

Judy is not the exception among film team members, she is more the rule. Her pioneering spirit and positive, God-oriented goals, her love for people and her dedication to advancing the gospel are traits that so many demonstrate as they work together taking the film *JESUS* into country after country.

In light of all they face, it could be hard to understand why a bright, eager college student or business-person might sacrifice vacation time, or take a leave of absence from a lucrative job to spend their time as part of a *JESUS* film team. Judy George explains it best.

"People are lost without the Lord, and if *we* don't help them know Him, maybe nobody else will. When I help train Filipino students to share their faith, I can see the results. Entire villages are reached for the first time with the message of God's love, *and I've had something to do with that.*"

She flashes a quick, contagious smile. "It's not always easy," she says, "but I've never been bored! This life is rewarding beyond anything I've ever experienced." Judy looks toward the mountain where she spent her summer with the team, then adds thoughtfully, "I never understood how great the Lord is until I had nobody to rely on but Him."

CHAPTER EIGHTEEN
ONE LAST CHANCE

Joe Balraj finally steered his little car around the bulging bus that had lumbered ahead of us for the last ten miles. People were squeezed into every possible inch of the vehicle as it swayed and lurched down the road from Madras, spitting black smoke into the humid air. But passing the bus changed very little on this typical Indian road.

The crumbling pavement was pocked with holes and ruts from the constant use of animals and vehicles of every conceivable size and description. Mammoth trucks burdened down with tons of granite pulverized what was left of the pavement as they rolled impatiently along the road, part of a steady stream of straw-laden oxcarts, push carts, bicycles, motor scooters and independent, unschooled animals. In the midst of the confusion wanders an assortment of cows, caribou, oxen, and small children driving geese and goats toward some far-off green pastureland. And all of it is mixed with the everpresent dust and stifling heat and humidity.

Joe, the local coordinator for the showings of *JESUS*, pulled around an oxcart and stopped the car next to a

soupy irrigation ditch. "We've shown the film in eighteen
villages in this area," he said. "This is one of them."

I followed his gaze out the dust-laden window toward
a scattered settlement of thatched roof huts.

"There are about five hundred people who live here,
Paul. Before we showed the film seven weeks ago there
were no known believers in this village. Last Sunday we
baptized a hundred and thirty-eight. All of them found
Christ through the film, and we've established a prayer
cell which meets in that little shack over there.

"New believers meet there three or four times a week
to pray and read the Bible," he went on. "The Church
of South India is trying to send them a pastor, but in the
meantime one of our village evangelists meets with them
twice a week to help them grow in their faith." He opened
the car door. "C'mon," he said, "I want you to meet
some of them."

Each person I talked to said they had decided to follow
Christ after seeing *JESUS* because it was the first time
they had heard how to know God. And that is what they
wanted: to know God.

One young couple I spoke with invited me into their
home. It was a painfully crude shack and it was easy to
see they did not have much. When I asked them what it
was they liked most about Jesus, the man said, "He cares
about poor people like us." Softly his wife added, "I
knew He was poor like we are because He never carried
a suitcase."

Another couple smiled and said, "We have been so
worried because we owe others a great deal of money.
But when we saw the picture, we learned that Jesus said
that if He took care of the birds and flowers of the field,
He would also take care of us. We still are not sure how

we will repay our debts, but we know Jesus will help us find a way."

The next new believer I met was Samuel. Samuel was in his eighties, sporting a few short, white hairs on the sides of his head, and peering at me through round spectacles taped to broken frames. His brown, leathery skin hung in folds around his thin frame, and he dressed in a few pieces of dingy white muslin. At a quick glance, he could have passed for Gandhi. Samuel had lived in this sad little village all his eighty years, but now he knew Jesus.

"I let some of my children become Christians," he told me, "but I was always against it. Then when I saw the *JESUS* film, I understood for the first time in my life that Jesus never died for Himself — *He died for me!* When I learned that, I knew I had to accept Him." He shook his head, as if angry with time. "If I had received Christ when I was young we would have a big congregation here, and a church." He looked me in the eyes and said in a strong voice, "We need a church and a pastor. Can you get them for us?"

As I was getting ready to leave, Samuel grabbed my arm. "My Hindu name used to be Muni Swami. That means 'little guru.'" He smiled broadly, "But, I was baptized last Sunday and my Christian name is Samuel."

I will remember Samuel.

"He'll get sick someday soon," Joe said. "He'll die, because there's no medical help around here. But now he knows Jesus."

It came late in his life, but Samuel had a chance to hear the message, and he believed.

* * *

Evening was fast approaching as we drove through

the gates of Mother Teresa's home for the abandoned and dying, just outside the city of Bangalore, India. We were greeted warmly by the home director, a gracious Sister with a radiant smile. Despite the dust and dirt everywhere in India, the Sister looked crisp and fresh in her pale blue habit, an "angel of mercy" to those she helps.

As she led us through the complex, I was not prepared for what we saw. In two small buildings were gathered two hundred and forty of the most pitiable human beings I have ever seen: crippled, diseased, retarded, senile — victims of life itself. Here were the unwanted, the wretched, the neglected and abandoned, whom life had laughed at and left to die alone.

Everywhere it was the same: roaming skeletons with black, sunken eyes, people missing limbs, old men and small children crippled and deformed beyond belief. The sounds and smells of the sick and dying were everywhere we looked. Yet quietly, gracefully moving among them, calling each by name and caring gently for their needs were the Sisters.

A few months before my visit they had shown the *JESUS* film to these people. Many had placed their faith in Christ. When we mentioned the film, faces lit up. Even those who could not speak shared what was on their hearts: By pressing their index fingers into the palms of their hands, then pointing to themselves they testified to the fact that Jesus had died for them.

Between the showing of the film and my visit, more than sixty who saw it had died, but for them there had been one last chance.

* * *

David Dass has used the film to work among the lepers. "Most of our work is in the slums and in the seven leper colonies within a few miles of here," he told me. There has been an encouraging response among the lepers, in particular the children.

"Many of the children contract the disease from their parents," he said, "mainly because they already suffer from malnutrition and their resistance is run down. We feed them porridge every morning to try to build them up physically and to try to prevent the spread of the leprosy. We have shown the *JESUS* film here because we so strongly believe they deserve one last chance."

* * *

The beautiful, romantic South Pacific has not always been so. In the 1870s and '80s missionaries in leaking sailing ships braved cyclones and hurricanes to bring the gospel to these islands. In the Fiji Islands in 1880, the first missionary to take the gospel there was killed and eaten by cannibals. But in 1981, *JESUS* film teams returned to the same islands to show the film to the descendants of those cannibals.

Among those who came forward after the picture was a 105-year-old man who had been alive when the missionary was killed. With tears coursing down his cheeks, he cried, "God is so good! He allowed me to live one hundred years so I could find Jesus."

But for others, there is not much time. In the disease-ridden refugee camps of Africa, every sunrise reveals another group of lifeless bodies, men and women who did not make it through the night.

In a gray and hopeless prison in Port Sudan the invitation to receive Christ was given after the showing of the film. Would these hardened convicts be open to such a simple message? Of the one hundred twenty who attended, eighty desired to know Christ.

One who responded was a man who had killed five people. He could not understand how God could forgive him until he saw the gospel explained clearly on the screen. He wept openly as he received Christ, and he said afterward that he could die without being afraid because he had peace in his heart. He knew the first face he would see after his execution would be the face of Jesus. A few days later he was shot by a firing squad.

The breath of the Spirit of God is blowing fresh across the world. We are in the midst of the greatest harvest of the centuries, reaping the results of the work of faithful men and women of God who have gone before us. But the harvest is great and the workers are far too few . . . unless you and I are willing to live our lives on the edge of a miracle doing whatever is necessary so that one more village can hear.

CHAPTER NINETEEN
TO THE ENDS
OF THE EARTH

They came from the deep canyons and rough-hewn caves of the Sierra Madre Occidental Mountains of Mexico. A tribe of primitive people, practically untouched by the changes of time, the Tarahumaras used witchcraft and animal sacrifices, drunken dancing and the symbol of the cross to appease the god Onoruame and seek his protection from lightning, fires and flood.

In the hillside clearing, two hundred men, women and children sat silently watching *JESUS*, the only film in the world translated into the Tarahumara language. It had taken months of work and twenty thousand dollars to complete the project.

The voice of the narrator belonged to Eduardo Lopes. Eduardo had been born and raised in the village of Samachique and was no stranger to translation work. In 1942, his father Ramon, had begun working with Wycliffe missionary, Kenneth Hilton, on a translation of the New Testament. Thirty years later the first Tarahumara New Testament was printed, but its reception was cool. Ramon and a few others had accepted Christ but in a total population of seventy-five thousand, Christians numbered less than one hundred. In 1975, just after the New Testaments arrived in Samachique, Hilton returned to North America.

Nearly ten years later, Eric and Terri Powell, field staff with the Navajo Gospel Mission, initiated the Tarahumara film production based on Hilton's work. Jim Bowman, a businessman with film background from Tucson, Arizona, had traveled to Samachique in August, 1984, and recorded the narration track with Eduardo and Ramon, promising to return with the completed film and a team to show it in the mountain villages.

Ramon was skeptical. He had pastored the local church for many years and had seen North Americans come and go. Most of their promises of help and materials had not been kept, and when eight silent months passed after he and his son recorded the sound track, he had begun to believe the *JESUS* film would never reach their village. When the film team finally did arrive in Samachique, Ramon was distant and reserved.

Now as the crowd watched the film under the star-filled Mexican sky, team members scanned the faces, looking for responses. The people were visibly shaken by the cruelty and pain they witnessed as Jesus was put to death on the cross. One man became physically ill. The burial scenes seemed to impress them, and the team learned later that the Tarahumara fear death deeply, sending their dead to the afterlife with days of elaborate ceremonies. They had seen many similarities between their burial customs and the Jewish ways in Jesus' time.

When the film ended, Ramon asked those interested in knowing more about Jesus to come to the lights stretched across the front of the film site. Christians in the group were praying for those they knew needed Christ, but no

one came. Finally, deeply disappointed that no one had
responded to the message, Ramon and the others wandered
off to their caves and their roughly built shacks.

Everyone had gone except a few who clustered around
the fires the team had built on the edges of the clearing.
Twenty-five or thirty Tarahumaras warmed themselves in
small groups, talking quietly, as if waiting for something.
All of the Christians — those who spoke Tarahumara —
had left, and team members were forced to speak with
the seekers in Spanish. Only a few teenaged boys understood any Spanish, but they stayed, asking questions.

Why had the people not come to the lights when
Ramon invited them? It was later very clear that the
invitation made them feel singled out. In their culture the
only time a person is set apart from the group is for
punishment or tribal ostracism. The team adjusted and
asked people to stay afterward around the fires, or to raise
their hands if they wanted to know more about receiving
Christ. In the four days they spent with the Tarahumaras,
more than eight hundred viewed the film, with an estimated
95 percent never having heard the gospel before. More
than eighty people responded to the message.

During the day the people returned to talk with the
team about spiritual things. One young man who had seen
the film said he had not slept all night — he did not
know what to do with Jesus. Others asked where the
people came from who had killed Jesus, and one wanted
answers about the sacrifice Jesus made for us. Jim Bowman
asked him about the sacrifices he made.

"I must offer goats, burros and chickens to Onoruame
so that my crops will not fail and God will not be angry
with me," he said.

"That's what Jesus has done for us," Jim said. "He

was the last sacrifice needed for all men, for all time."

The young man nodded, and a smile spread across his face. "I understand!" he said. "For the first time I understand what Jesus did for us."

In Choquita a Spanish-speaking Mexican missionary hosted a showing of the film, and was thrilled to see the Tarahumaras he had been trying to communicate with understanding and responding to the message. Ten men raised their hands indicating they were asking God to forgive their sins.

With each day's showing of the film Ramon and the other Christians were encouraged. The film opened avenues for distribution of many of the Tarahumara New Testaments found in Kenneth Hilton's old house. A few of the older men and many of the young men could read, and *JESUS* had caused questions and created an interest in them that had not existed before. By the time the team packed up their gear and headed homeward, Ramon was making plans for more showings of the *JESUS* film in other Tarahumara villages.

* * *

It was late, and the moon hung low and bright over the Caribbean as we struggled against the waves threatening to capsize our dugout canoe. Warm winds blew hard through the palms on shore, churning the sea to a tempest while the thirty-five horsepower outboard strained to pull us through. Several inches of water sloshed around us and our equipment, and I watched the two native boys bail it back over the side as fast as their young arms could manage. There were no oars, no moon, and no life jackets and I prayed earnestly that God would get us to shore.

We were headed along the coast of Honduras with

missionary David Dickson bound for a Garifuna village where the gospel had never been shared. *JESUS* was scheduled to be screened for hundreds of Black Caribs in the language of the Garifuna Indians, and we did not plan to disappoint them. Finally, we headed the canoe toward shore and were soon unloading on an isolated beach.

In a tropical paradise that stretches along the coast of Honduras, Guatemala, Belize and Nicaragua, one hundred thousand Black Caribs coax their livelihood from the sea as fishermen. Descendants of 19th century black Africans who escaped from slave ships and settled with the Carib Indians, they have been almost overlooked by those with the Good News — but not quite. In 1955 a young Wycliffe translator named Lillian Howland went to Central America to begin translation work on the New Testament. Thirty years later she completed the translation but few Garifunas had responded to the gospel. David Dickson heard that she had mastered the language and began to study it under her tutelage and is now the only white man to speak it fluently. As he learned the language, his burden to see the Garifunas reached increased. He saw the *JESUS* film as an opportunity to spread the message quickly.

In 1984, David and two Garifunas left the palm-lined beaches and jungles of Honduras and flew to San Bernardino, California, to dub the film into their language. A few months later our team returned with the film ready to be shown to the Black Caribs.

In one scene Jesus greets a small child with a greeting known only to these people. "What are you doing?" Jesus' Garifuna voice says. "Nothing," the child responds, and the Black Carib audiences break into applause and delighted laughter. "This man knows Garifuna!" someone says. "He speaks our language. He knows our greeting!"

As the film progressed, Dickson moved among the

crowd of two hundred chattering people to hear what was being said about the film. When Jesus healed someone, comments like, "Look at that! Can you believe that!" were heard. One woman said to her friend, "Who wouldn't believe in Jesus? Did you see Him heal that blind man? Anyone would want to believe in Him."

The Garifunas were especially pleased with scenes that involved the sea and the fisherman's way of life. They loved watching Peter and the disciples haul straining nets filled with fish into their boats. And when Jesus spoke to the winds and calmed the sea, everyone in the audience related to what they saw because all of them had lost family and friends who drowned in angry storms at sea.

They talked throughout the entire film, but the message got through. After the showing, fifteen men and twenty women gathered under the lights to make decisions to trust Christ. On the final evening, the team showed the film in a large village to a crowd of eighteen hundred Garifunas. Everyone came — drunks, unruly children, even witch doctors performing incantations as the film was shown. But the Spirit of God is strong enough to meet any challenge, and that night one hundred fifty-five made decisions for Christ.

The need is there — an insatiable hunger for the God of love. And through the film *JESUS*, the message is being told and understood. On our three-day trip to the Garifunas two hundred of them prayed to receive Christ. Churches are being established, disciples are being made, and their faith is being built up. "Come back," a Garifuna village chief said. "You must come back again and tell us more about Christ."

This year David Dickson will take the film to forty more villages. He believes that as many as ten thousand

may respond to the message. The Garifuna and the Tarahumara Indians have been called "unreached people." The
JESUS film may be the key to reaching them and thousands
of other groups like them around the world.

EPILOGUE:

PLANS, HOPES AND DREAMS

If I could choose any time in which to be alive, this would be the time! We are beginning to see the fulfillment of the prophecies of Matthew 24, and we are in one of the most exciting times in human history!

Before Jesus ascended into heaven, His disciples asked Him what would take place just before His return to earth. He gave a number of signs including an increase in earthquakes, lawlessness, and wars. But in the fourteenth verse of that chapter He says, "This gospel of the kingdom shall be preached for a witness to all the nations, and then the end will come."

Several years ago I sat down with one of the vice-presidents of the Coca-Cola Bottling Company and discussed some of their objectives. I discovered that day that they have a plan to take Coca Cola to every person in the world. And they are doing it! Contracts they have signed in China make it possible for another billion people to be reached by Coke.

They are dead serious about their objectives and are giving their lives for this cause. If you were to go to their corporate headquarters in Atlanta you would find that they can tell you how many countries they are working in, how many wholesale and retail outlets they have, how many people hear the message of Coke each day, and how many people take Coca-Cola into their lives every day. Their marketing plan is extraordinary.

But we are "marketing" a "product" that changes lives for eternity, and I consider my involvement in laying the plans for the continued translation and distribution of the *JESUS* film to be one of the greatest privileges of my life.

We are strategists for Christ, thinking of new ways to reach people with the message of life. You have read just a few results of the film, only a few. Look now with me at our strategy and plans. Check our progress. And while you look, perhaps the Lord will show you where you might play a part in the future of the world.

* * *

The Need for Evangelistic Films like JESUS

There are two major reasons why we need a film which accurately and simply draws people to the Lord:

1. *Almost half the world is illiterate or only marginally literate.* In 1980, UNESCO reported that nearly 30 percent of the world's population was illiterate, over seven hundred thirty-six *million* adults. In addition, another 20 percent have so little education that they are almost functionally illiterate. Written materials are completely ineffective with these groups.

2. *God has prepared the hearts of men and women all over the world to receive His Son.* Millions of people would receive Christ now if given the opportunity, but we who are His people must take the message to them.

Translation Goals

1. Our first objective will be to translate the film into the world's major languages. In 1982, David Barrett published the *World Christian Encyclopedia* in which are listed 271 major languages (those that have more than one million speakers). Our first goal then, is to produce a lip-sync translation for each of these languages. If the Lord does not return soon, these translations can be used for generations because of the timelessness of the film. At this writing we have completed over one hundred translations, but hundreds of languages remain, and the cost is nearly $20,000 apiece.

2. Our second objective is to continue to produce story-telling or narration versions in the smaller languages and dialects as funds become available. A narration version can be produced for about $10,000.

3. Third, we want to assist other mission organizations who request the film for use among small people groups. We will provide them with the technical elements and sound tracks at our cost.

4. Fourth, we would like to ensure that a package of follow-up materials is available for each language that the film is dubbed into. Wherever people are literate, we want to leave written Scriptures and other materials that clearly tell how to receive Christ, how to be filled with the Holy Spirit, and how to grow in personal faith. Literature packets cost about $6,000 to translate.

5. Fifth, we will make the *JESUS* film available to Bible translators in order to assist them in their work with new languages.

* * *

The Distribution Plan

Motion Picture Theaters. Wherever possible, we will initiate a film run in theaters. This helps to give the picture stature in a country, and newspaper advertising in major cities helps to create awareness of the film and leads to larger crowds for the 16mm showings.

National Television. This is a major strategy because it reaches a different group of people. In media-saturated western countries, theater runs are short, making TV a viable alternative for exposing many to the film. In the developing countries of the Third World, however, only government leaders or the wealthy can afford a television. This group urgently needs to be reached and is often neglected.

Cable Television. This is an alternative method for exposing the film on a continuing basis. Year after year, *JESUS* is shown during Christmas and Easter seasons on some of the major cable networks in North America.

16mm Film Teams. Though much more costly, this method of distribution provides for more thorough follow-up than theater and television options. Screening locations can be established in rural areas, and the personal involvement provides maximum follow-up for new believers.

Our goal is to field five thousand film teams by 1995. This will be one team for every one million people in the world. Each team can show the film to about two hundred thousand people per year or one million people over a five-year period. To fully equip a team with projector, generator, screen, lights and microphone, costs $3,000 per team, plus the cost of the film print at $1,200, plus shipping and customs fees. (More than nine thousand copies of the film are needed now.) In addition, each team needs $2,000 a month for operating expenses.

Videotapes. One of the fastest growing media phenomenon around the world is the use of videocassette recorders. Our videocassette strategy has three main thrusts:

1. To make English videotapes widely available in North America for the purpose of raising funds to expand in the rest of the world.

2. To provide videocassettes of the film in minority languages, which could be used to reach immigrants. For instance, in North America, Christians could invite Haitians or Cambodians into their homes to show them the film in their mother tongue.

3. To place foreign-language cassettes in video rental shops frequented by immigrants. For example, there are two million Turks living in Germany. Our objective would be to make *JESUS* available in a Turkish translation at those shops frequented by Turks.

Follow-up and Church Planting. The *JESUS* film is only one component in an overall plan to see millions of new believers become true disciples of our Lord and follow Him in fellowship with a local church. As its part of the overall strategy we have five major objectives:

1. To broadly expose millions of people to the life and claims of Jesus Christ.

2. To see an explosion in church growth through the effective follow-up of new converts.

3. To sow the seed of the gospel broadly, and to be alert to where the Holy Spirit is preparing hearts, and thus be more effective in placing full-time workers.

4. To challenge pastors of local churches to train their laymen in personal evangelism and follow-up as a prerequisite to sponsoring film showings in their area.

5. To provide a visual confirmation and credibility

to the Christian message in areas where it has previously been considered myth and folklore.

From country to country, culture to culture, the *JESUS* film, like the Scripture from which it is taken, meets the needs of man. A moonshine bootlegger in southern Kenya told me one morning, "I always thought that the story of Jesus was a myth, but last night I saw the film and I know it is true. I have asked Him to come into my life now."

Technology can be used around the world to preach truth or tell lies. In our materialistic, hedonistic western world, the media teaches us that we are self-sufficient and self-reliant and that morality is relative. Through this film, many are now being shown that true fulfillment can be found only in Jesus.

One of the vital links in the follow-up plans for the *JESUS* film is the establishment of what are called New Life Training Centers. Here believers receive vision, strategy, and training in helping to fulfill the Great Commission.

Organized in centrally located churches, believers come for a month at a time to be equipped for personal evangelism, follow-up and discipleship. During the morning hours they study the Scriptures and learn how to teach them to others. The afternoons are given to personal evangelism; the evenings are used for showing the *JESUS* film.

Each participating layman must develop a specific strategy of evangelism and discipleship for his home church. This strategy includes forming a house fellowship for those he has led to Christ and for those who have received Christ through the *JESUS* film and other mass evangelistic efforts. Each Home Bible Fellowship has the potential of becoming a "daughter" church.

Today many people are coming to Christ in areas where there are no Christian churches. Between 1976 and 1983 the number of believers in Nepal grew from five hundred to more than fifteen thousand baptized believers. Approximately 90 percent of these believers meet in homes. Yet, there are not even ten leaders for two hundred fifty-eight churches and Home Bible Fellowships.

During the past year, thirty-seven new leaders have been trained for these fellowships along with more than one hundred laymen. During the first year of operation, the teams of the Patan, Nepal, training center personally shared the gospel with six thousand Nepalese.

The *JESUS* film works hand in hand with the training center, local churches, missionaries, and the whole body of Christ to be a tool of evangelism in the presentation of the gospel.

The impact of the *JESUS* film is just beginning. It is as timeless as Scripture itself, for that is what it is. It is Scripture brought to life. And wherever it is shown — even in prisons of oppressive regimes — it brings freedom. I shall never forget the words of Alexandar Solzhenitsyn as he spoke of true freedom in *The Gulag Archipelago*, "Bless you, prison, for having been in my life."[1]

Malcolm Muggeridge, the great writer and philosopher, was fascinated by Solzhenitsyn's statement. "It was in prison that he discovered what real freedom was," Muggeridge says. "In one of the most brutal prisons of Russia, he watched the man in the bunk above who had discovered true freedom. This fellow somehow in that terrible place remained cheerful, remained brotherly, remained helpful to others. Solzhenitsyn observed that in the evening, when this man crawled into his bunk, he pulled some pieces of paper out of his pocket and started reading them. They were sentences scribbled, and, of course, came from the Gospels. I thought when I read this: Have any other sentences in all human history been written that could also have comforted and uplifted a man in that terrible place? Suppose they had been sentences from the Charter of the United Nations. Do you imagine they would have given that man one moment's peace in the circumstances in which he was placed? That's what we have to remember, that we find freedom not in courts of law or in international declarations. We find freedom in our relations with our Creator and through the Incarnation of Jesus as recorded in the Gospels."

When asked to make a prediction as to what would happen in the future, Muggeridge said this: "I am no prophet, I am a journalist. If, however, I were to venture upon an essay in prophecy, it would be this — whatever may happen to the nightmare utopias of the twentieth century, whether they mutually destroy one another or, metaphorically speaking, fall into one another's arms, however deep the darkness that may fall upon our world, of one thing we may be certain. In some forgotten jungle a naked savage will feel impelled to daub a stone with colored mud and prostrate himself before it, thereby opening yet another chapter in man's everlasting and indefatigable quest for God, making one more humble acknowledgment of his existence and his destiny."

The *JESUS* film is helping scores of missions each year to present the claims of Christ to millions who have not yet found freedom in Christ. It is a tool that God has given to the whole body of Christ, not just one organization. It is our privilege to serve over one hundred missions currently. Far beyond entertainment, the film evangelizes, edifies, teaches and makes disciples.

If you would like to be informed of the continuing impact of the film, to know current needs and receive updated reports, write to:

THE JESUS PROJECT
Campus Crusade for Christ
Arrowhead Springs 40-50
San Bernardino, CA 92414

or call (714) 495-7383.

This story is not finished. We will know the final results only when we see Jesus face to face. That day is coming! And just maybe the Lord will use this film to help bring many more into the Kingdom before His return. That is my heartfelt prayer!

[1] Aleksandr I. Solzhenitsyn, *The Gulag Archipelago* (New York: Harper and Row, 1973).

Dear Paul,

I've been encouraged by reading your book, "I Just Saw Jesus," and I want to respond to your challenge and take a greater part in helping to fulfill the Great Commission.

 I want to hear more stories about how God is using the "JESUS" film around the world and want to be encouraged in my faith. Please send me your quarterly newsletter, The Jesus Project UPDATE. SL1170

Please send me information on how I can join The Jesus Project NETWORK of monthly donors, a team of men and women committed to helping take the "JESUS" film into new areas. I understand that all NETWORK funds are used to meet the most urgent needs of The Jesus Project. SL1170

I want to pray about being a part of some of the things described in your book. Please send me information about joining a short-term summer project showing the "JESUS" film. JTF

Sincerely _____

Address _____

_____

_____

2571535/N6N002

Dear Paul,

I've been encouraged by reading your book, "I Just Saw Jesus," and I want to respond to your challenge and take a greater part in helping to fulfill the Great Commission.

 I want to hear more stories about how God is using the "JESUS" film around the world and want to be encouraged in my faith. Please send me your quarterly newsletter, The Jesus Project UPDATE. SL1170

Please send me information on how I can join The Jesus Project NETWORK of monthly donors, a team of men and women committed to helping take the "JESUS" film into new areas. I understand that all NETWORK funds are used to meet the most urgent needs of The Jesus Project. SL1170

I want to pray about being a part of some of the things described in your book. Please send me information about joining a short-term summer project showing the "JESUS" film. JTF

Sincerely _____

Address _____

_____

_____

2571535/N6N002

THE **JESUS** PROJECT

P.O. Box 7690
Laguna Niguel, CA 92677

THE **JESUS** PROJECT

P.O. Box 7690
Laguna Niguel, CA 92677

Dear Paul,

I've been encouraged by reading your book, "I Just Saw Jesus," and I want to respond to your challenge and take a greater part in helping to fulfill the Great Commission.

 I want to hear more stories about how God is using the "JESUS" film around the world and want to be encouraged in my faith. Please send me your quarterly newsletter, The Jesus Project UPDATE. SL1170

☐ Please send me information on how I can join The Jesus Project NETWORK of monthly donors, a team of men and women committed to helping take the "JESUS" film into new areas. I understand that all NETWORK funds are used to meet the most urgent needs of The Jesus Project. SL1170

☐ I want to pray about being a part of some of the things described in your book. Please send me information about joining a short-term summer project showing the "JESUS" film. JTF

Sincerely _____
Address _____
_____
_____

2571535/N6N002

Dear Paul,

I've been encouraged by reading your book, "I Just Saw Jesus," and I want to respond to your challenge and take a greater part in helping to fulfill the Great Commission.

 I want to hear more stories about how God is using the "JESUS" film around the world and want to be encouraged in my faith. Please send me your quarterly newsletter, The Jesus Project UPDATE. SL1170

☐ Please send me information on how I can join The Jesus Project NETWORK of monthly donors, a team of men and women committed to helping take the "JESUS" film into new areas. I understand that all NETWORK funds are used to meet the most urgent needs of The Jesus Project. SL1170

☐ I want to pray about being a part of some of the things described in your book. Please send me information about joining a short-term summer project showing the "JESUS" film. JTF

Sincerely _____
Address _____
_____
_____

2571535/N6N002

THE **JESUS** PROJECT

P.O. Box 7690
Laguna Niguel, CA 92677

THE **JESUS** PROJECT

P.O. Box 7690
Laguna Niguel, CA 92677